D0909090

KABBALAH ON Sleep

Kabbalah Publishing is a registered DBA of Kabbalah Centre International, Inc.

For further information:

The Kabbalah Centre
155 E. 48th St., New York, NY 10017
1062 S. Robertson Blvd., Los Angeles, CA 90035

1.800.Kabbalah   www.kabbalah.com

First Edition
March 2009
Printed in USA
ISBN13: 978-1-57189-620-9

Design: HL Design (Hyun Min Lee) www.hldesignco.com

KABBALAH ON

Sleep

YEHUDA BERG

TABLE OF CONTENTS

Part One

The Phenomenon of Sleep and the Power of Night

The Purpose of Sleep

There is a reason for the existence of day and night, sun and moon, light and darkness, sleep and wakefulness. In fact, there is a reason for *everything* that exists—from a handful of sand grains on a Honolulu beach to a supernova in deep space. The ancient source of wisdom known as Kabbalah explains that everything in our physical universe, including the laws of physics, are the reflection of a higher truth, a force of energy (or consciousness) that exists beyond the realm of the five senses.

Understanding the root spiritual force that is the underlying DNA of physical phenomena allows us to gain access to that force, and to use it as a means for transforming ourselves, and for transforming our world.

Nothing exists by chance. Nothing. The fact that night, darkness, sleep, and dreams are part of the human experience means they are a reflection of some higher truth. Night has a purpose. Sleep has a purpose. Life has a purpose. If one does not know what it is, how can we take steps to ensure the purpose is achieved? We can't. Life simply becomes a random process of trial and error, mindless, chaotic, and meaningless. Sound familiar?

The ancient sages of Kabbalah devoted their lifetimes to revealing the true Purpose of Creation so that humankind could grasp the meaning of existence, and therefore bring about the ultimate objective: Nothing less than unending life, happiness, and joy, far beyond what we might dare to imagine.

Sleep, sexual relations, and sunbathing on a glorious day at the beach all offer a microscopic taste of the future age of Messiah, a time when death and chaos will be eradicated from the landscape of human existence. Such transcendent moments lift us out of the hectic, noisy, turbulent experiences which mark life on Earth. Sleep provides us with a respite from the commotion and chaos of human existence, but it also serves a much deeper purpose. The *Zohar*, the most important text of Kabbalah, and the great kabbalists themselves, offer us a look into the profound value and true purpose of this unique phenomenon we call sleep.

Chapter One

Welcome to the True Reality

We believe that the world around us represents reality, while the dream world we inhabit when we sleep is illusory, an imaginary creation of our resting brain. Not so, according to Kabbalah. Time and space and physical matter are the illusions, perpetuated by the physical senses. When we sleep, we leave the illusionary world around us and enter into a dimension that Kabbalah describes as an authentic reality.

To our senses our dreams feel imagined, and what we experience when we're awake seems to be real. However, if you look more deeply into the material world, you poke a hole in the fabric of physicality and you begin to see it for what it is: A mirage. According to the *Zohar*, the physical world is a simulation run on a software program equipped with its own set of physical laws. And if you look further into the simulation, you will see that these laws are not real.

For instance, if you probe deeper into our virtual reality you will discover that time and space are not separate entities but one. You also discover that time flowing ever forward is an illusion. This view simply does not hold up when you probe the microscopic level of our world, where the direction of time also flows in reverse.

It's funny. Einstein was the one who told us that time and space are really one entity, which he dubbed the *space-time continuum*. However, some 2000 years *before* Einstein, ancient kabbalists made the exact same statement. Interestingly, Einstein and contemporary physicists still have no working explanation for this phenomenon we call time, although they readily acknowledge that it is an illusion. They also understand that at the level of molecules and atoms, time moves both forward and backward, even though time reversal does not seem to take place in the reality we all perceive.

But if atoms can travel back and forth in time, why can't we do the same, since we are just a bunch of atoms? What's going on here?

Time, according to Kabbalah, is defined as the distance between Cause and Effect. In the realm of true reality,

Cause and Effect happen simultaneously, and thus there is no such thing as time. In our everyday world, Cause and Effect, action and reaction, are separated by time (and space). However, when we sleep and dream, time has no physical effect on our experiences, as we'll soon explore. The fact that dreams are not governed by the rules of time is further evidence that when we sleep we are closer to Kabbalah's true reality.

According to the *Zohar*, time is a manifestation of the concept of mercy. What does this mean? For every negative Cause or seed that we plant, there will be a negative Effect or consequence. If there were no such thing as time, negative actions would yield an *immediate* negative response. If time did not exist, the consequence of an action would be in our face the moment we performed that action.

For instance, if every time we uttered an unkind word about a friend or an enemy, we immediately felt the pain our words caused, we'd stop gossiping and bad-mouthing others in a hurry. Unfortunately, this change in our behavior would be motivated by fear of an immediate painful response. This kind of change in behavior is no different from what happens when we train an animal. We are not animals. In order to give human beings ownership of our own transformations, Cause and Effect were separated by time, giving birth to free will, the one distinguishing feature between the animal kingdom and humankind.

In our everyday existence, we do not experience an immediate consequence of our positive and negative deeds. Good deeds are not rewarded on the spot. Rotten behavior is not met with immediate payback. This creates the powerful illusion of injustice, chaos, luck, and chance. Time delays the repercussions of all our deeds, and this delay can often last months, years, decades, and even lifetimes.

Time and the illusion of chaos it perpetuates allow us to *choose* to change, to transform using our own free will. Even our doubt about time's purpose, and the delay of every consequence, is there to manufacture the opportunity for free will. Although you are now discovering the purpose of time, the very existence of time prevents us from grasping this knowledge with profound understanding and total conviction. If we did, we'd lose our free will. If we truly perceived the function and essence of time, we would see the end in the beginning of every deed. However, you can be sure that to whatever degree we now accept, embrace, and understand the role of time, this is enough to provide us with the right amount of free will to become the Cause and creators of the infinite joy that will be ours once we complete our transformation.

Let's see how this idea of time as mercy relates to the concept of sleep.

TIME AS MERCY

One reason why time is referred to as the manifestation of mercy is that it gives us an opportunity to sidestep negative consequences and avert judgments that are due us. How? By changing. By transforming. If we change, if we uproot and eradicate the particular selfish trait that motivated our behavior in the first place, then we do not have to experience its payback. Every Cause does not have to have the same Effect upon us.

This is why time is merciful. It gives us an opportunity to deflect judgment. Keep in mind that inner change is not just a promise to God, or a well-intentioned pledge to our loved ones that we will mend our ways. There are no promises in the world of Kabbalah. There are only results. Actions. Deeds. Hence, you can only avoid judgment with a bona fide transformation of character that is permanent. There is no fooling the universe. You cannot deceive the physical laws of nature or the spiritual laws of nature. If the change is real, then the inherent metaphysical Laws of the Universe, by design, prevent judgment from striking. It is automatic. It is the law.

The judgment of the universe is not a decision made by God, or a verdict handed down by some divine court, so there is no reason to pray to God for forgiveness. True prayer harnesses the Divine Energy that radiates from the Creator in order to cleanse us of our negative, self-centered qualities. This is what forgiveness and prayer are really all about. As we'll soon see, sleep plays a role in this process as well.

We now understand that we alone answer our own prayers by virtue of changing. Change. Only change. That is the key to everything. The world doesn't change when people don't change. The same pain, suffering, hurt, and chaos inflict this world today as they have for the last 20 centuries because people are the same—inside. When a person achieves the improbable—inner transformation and recognition of his or her stupidity of ego and selfishness—the universe is hardwired to redirect judgments another way. We're off the hook. We've avoided a nasty fate.

However, there is still some karmic debt that is due, a tear in the fabric of the cosmos that must be repaired. Thankfully, because of our transformation, we do not have to endure the payback in this physical reality. There is a more merciful way to pay back the debt.

It is called *sleep*.

Chapter Two

Sleep and the Taste of Death

THE POWER OF SLEEP

When we sleep, our soul—the true self—rises out of the realm of time and space, out of our physical body, and enters true reality. In a dream, time has no physical hold over us. This is why we can wake up after dozing and think we've been dreaming for hours, when it turns out to have been just a few moments. This is a glimpse of true reality, unbound by the effects of time, space, and motion.

Because we are not shackled by physical limitations in a dream, we can be at two places at the same time, and experience a multitude of events simultaneously. We can be in one location one moment and halfway across the world the next. When we are in a dream, it feels as real as this present moment. But when we awake, we dismiss the events of the dream as fantasy, hallucination, or a figment of our sleeping imagination.

The fact is if we allowed ourselves to truly experience the reality we glimpse in our dreams, we would discover a mind-bending truth: This world is the dream state, and what we call a dream state is true reality! Right now we are all sleeping, and when we're asleep tonight we'll be truly awake.

Make no mistake; if you remembered your dreams as they really are (true reality), both realities—the dream state and the world you now perceive—would be indistinguishable from one another. True reality was concealed on purpose; the higher truths were dimmed so we could sojourn in this temporary, chaotic existence for the purpose of truly changing our character, and thereby earning the endless joy that is our destiny.

But for now, until we reach that egoless, unselfish state, our senses and our conscious minds are restricted and limited by design, and we interpret this other night-time, sleep-time reality as a faint dream, an illusion of the sleeping mind. We are only allowed to sense this true reality as a muted impression; it is there as a tool to assist us in our efforts toward transforming this painful nightmare of our everyday world into a blissful dream world of unending delight and fulfillment.

THE CORRECTION

One purpose of sleep is to allow us to pay back karmic debts in the dream state so that the pain associated with those spiritual corrections is not fully experienced in this physical world. Any pain, nightmare, or hurt that you suffer during a dream is usually a result of this Cause-and-Effect payback. Making a spiritual correction (*tikkun* in Hebrew, or *karma* in Sanskrit) in a dream is simply a more merciful way to achieve the objective.

This has tremendous benefits. Why? Think of spiritual corrections as a kind of major surgical procedure. During surgery a person goes under anesthesia to induce sleep so that the patient does not experience the pain and trauma of physical corrections. Imagine if you were forced to undergo surgery while being wide-awake! This is comparable to what's happening in our daily lives, so we're very fortunate to have sleep as an alternative.

The things we experience in a sleep state during childhood, up to the age of twelve for a girl and thirteen for a boy, are often associated with past-life experiences. According to Kabbalah, all of us bring some form of past-life baggage into this current life. For instance, children often experience night terrors, which are different from nightmares. A night terror is a moment of intense fear and sudden waking, which can include screaming or crying, sweating, and a rapid heart rate. No specific dream is recalled.

According to Kabbalah, a night terror is either a moment of payback; the cleansing of a negative deed performed in a previous life, or a memory of a past-life traumatic event, like sudden death, suffering, or pain. The complete memory of the experience is concealed from the conscious mind to lessen the pain of the individual—unlike a nightmare, which can be recalled in detail.

When we become adults, our dreams and nightmares are purification experiences related to negative actions we've taken in our *present* life. Of course, the fact that self-centered behavior carries the kinds of negative consequences we see in our dreams is mostly hidden from our rational minds. Once again, this concealment allows us to experience free will. Fortunately, Cause and Effect seem to be at work here, too: The more we seek to transform ourselves in the physical realm, the more opportunities we have to discharge our baggage and pay off our spiritual debts in a dream state.

Payback, as it occurs through the Universal Law of Cause and Effect, is not payback for its own sake. It serves a higher purpose. The pain of payback, however it appears in our life, purifies the ego. It's just that simple. It raises our consciousness. It has a transformative effect on who we are.

Pain changes us because sooner or later we get fed up with it, and we learn the lesson that pain conveys. If pain lasts, if chaos endures, it simply means we have not learned the right lesson and made the appropriate change in our character. Any chaos that still remains in our life, no matter what it is, is only there to pressure us into giving up some self-centered trait buried deep within us.

In the context of Kabbalah, there are two ways to transform. *Transformation* has a very specific definition: The eradication of the ego so that we *Receive for the Sake of Sharing*, as opposed to *Receiving for the Self Alone*. I will discuss, in greater detail, the often misunderstood *Desire to Receive for the Sake of Sharing* in just a moment. First, allow me to explain the two paths to transformation.

The Path of Pain: This is the path of trial and error. On this path, we listen to our ego and we follow it blindly in every area of our life. Time then delays the negative repercussions of our self-centered behavior, so that when they finally appear (usually when we least expect them) they seem totally random and feel like unjust suffering. Regardless of how it seems on the surface, pain does succeed in weakening the will of the body and of the ego. It will usually continue until we finally surrender and wave the white flag. The stronger the ego, the longer this process takes. Some people's pain has to become unbearable, and they are driven to their knees before they finally let go of the ego's directives.

The Path of Fulfillment: This alternative is the path of Kabbalah, where we proactively choose to transform. We study, practice, learn, and live Kabbalah, using every opportunity to recognize and let go of the influence of the ego (our Opponent, also known by the Hebrew word *Satan*, which means "opponent" or "adversary").

Letting go of ego is the most difficult task on Earth. Make no mistake about it. It is far easier to go off and fight in the army and experience the horrors of warfare than it is to let go completely of the human ego, which requires nothing less than spiritual warfare. Do you find it hard to believe that spiritual war is more difficult than physical war? A person will willingly step off a building, slit his wrists, hang himself in a room, or swallow a bottle of pills if his ego is damaged enough. When a man loses all his money, it is his ego that feels the pain, not the soul and true essence of the individual. All depression, anxiety, fear, panic, shame, embarrassment, and worry are simply different manifestations of ego, and these self-destructive emotions are powerful enough to drive a person to suicide.

The soul, our true self, never experiences such emotions. Never. Therefore, do not underestimate the power of ego, this formidable Opponent. However, the benefits of proactively choosing to undergo ego pain with the help of the technology of Kabbalah are many. First, *only the ego suffers* in this process. Our spiritual and physical well-being actually benefit. We experience untold joy as it relates to everything that money cannot buy—loving children, true friends, loving spouses, good health, genuine peace of mind, inner joy, lasting contentment, freedom from fear and anxiety, and all the necessities of life, including a happy home.

The pain necessary to transform us is experienced by the ego in both our everyday lives and during sleep, in our dreams, where the pain feels like just a bad dream. The reality of that pain is diminished so that it's usually just a faint memory upon waking—if we remember it at all. That's powerful stuff! What an amazing opportunity sleep offers us.

A DEEPER UNDERSTANDING OF THE *DESIRE TO RECEIVE*

Beginning students of Kabbalah know that the fundamental purpose of Kabbalah (and of life) is to transform our *Desire to Receive for the Self Alone* into the *Desire to Receive for the Sake of Sharing*. By delving more deeply into this central idea we can also better understand the role of sleep in the context of our lives.

The world is made up of atoms. According to science (and Kabbalah), what we experience as physical occurs because of the *electron*. Why? The electron, the negative force inside an atom, orbits the nucleus of the atom, vibrating so fast it creates the illusion of solidity we have come to know as physical matter, just as the rotors of a whirling fan create the illusion of a solid sphere. The electron is the negative force Kabbalah calls the consciousness of the Desire to *Receive for the Self Alone*. When we refer to the *Desire to Receive for the Self Alone* in this context, we are really just saying that the body (brought into being by the physical element known as the electron) exists simply to satisfy its own desire.

However, when we perform a genuine act of sharing (outside our comfort zone), what Kabbalah calls the *Desire to Receive (the body) for the Sake of Sharing* emerges. In other words, the body is being used to assist and care for others. It's that simple.

However, not everything that is simple is easy. When we consider using our bodies, our gifts, and our talents for the sake of sharing with other people instead of just for ourselves, we start to worry that we won't be able to take care of ourselves. But remember that more and more people reading books like this one are now working to share with you! Imagine millions of people concerned about you and sharing all of their talents and gifts with you. In a perfect world (which we are going to reach one way or another, either through suffering or transformation), we will all be doing exactly what we do now, with exactly the same level of talent.

The only difference will be a matter of consciousness. We'll be doing what we do for others instead of for ourselves.

When this simple switch in consciousness and action takes place, miracles beyond our imagining will erupt all over the planet. The *Zohar* tells us that death will lose its power, giving way to immortality. We will all enjoy never-ending happiness. Never-ending ecstasy.

How does all this relate to sleep? Allow me to share with you a story we often tell students all over the world. It's a well-known parable that concerns the difference between Heaven and Hell, and the role of consciousness therein. We can also use it to get a sense of the power of sleep and dreams.

HEAVEN VERSUS HELL

A student once asked his Kabbalah master to show him the difference between Heaven and Hell. When the student fell asleep later that night, the master transported his student to a lofty spiritual realm, whereupon the disciple was granted a vision that would reveal the answer to his question.

In his dream, the student saw a group of people gathered around a circular vat overflowing with an endless supply of potion that induced the most transcendent pleasure with every taste. However, each of the people at the vat had a giant spoon handcuffed to their wrists. They were able to dip their long-handled spoons into the vat to fill them with this divine concoction, but the length and size of the spoons kept the people from being able to turn the spoons around to their mouths so they could sip from them.

The resulting frustration was unbearable. This was Hell.

The student was now granted another vision. Strangely enough, the scene was almost identical. Once again, people were walking around a circular vat filled with the same potion that produced infinite ecstasy with each swallow. And, once again, the spoons and handles were oversized, handcuffed to the wrist of each person. At first the student was puzzled. How could this be Heaven, he wondered, when no one can fit the spoon into his or her mouth? But then he saw that each person simply fed the person in front of him. Everyone was experiencing a divine state of ecstasy beyond human comprehension.

The situation was the same, but the consciousness was different. The *Desire to Receive for the Self Alone,* which motivated those in Hell, caused untold anguish. Heaven was simply a matter of changing one's consciousness from receiving to sharing, so that everyone could enjoy infinite bliss. In Hell, everyone tried to feed themselves, and all they received was frustration; in Heaven, everyone fed someone else, and in this way all were fed.

Heaven is here now, without question. Paradise is right in front of our eyes. The Light never disappeared. It is only our *Desire to Receive for the Self Alone* that blinds us, preventing us from taking the simple step that leads to bliss and immortality. And until a critical mass of sharing consciousness is achieved, the power of unconditional sharing will remain concealed from our rational minds. Sure, we might understand it intellectually (as you do right now), but we cannot feel the transformative miracle that true sharing generates until we reach a critical mass.

The spiritual path of Kabbalah tells us that the power of sleep and dreams slowly but surely removes this blindfold. By giving us a taste of what it will be like when Divine Light fills our world, our sleeping life gradually weakens the deep-seated selfish impulses which govern our everyday thoughts and behaviors, and wakes us up to the promise of true reality.

THE POWER OF DEATH

People die for one reason, and one reason only. Death is a purification process. It weakens the ego and diminishes the will of the body, thereby cleansing us of the *Desire to Receive*. When we die, our consciousness (or soul) merely circulates until it forms another body in order to continue the process of transformation and spiritual growth.

Part of our consciousness may be directed into inanimate matter, or into the vegetable or animal kingdoms, depending on the corrections required by previous behaviors. But the vast majority of our consciousness (or soul) will form a new body. This occurs through the atoms which form the sperm and egg that will produce a baby. It occurs in a couple whose own consciousness (DNA, soul, or karma) will get passed on to the baby in the form of character traits—a process which will allow the soul to complete its particular inner transformation.

Of course, we do not remember any of this (to allow for free will), which means the idea of reincarnation may be met with skepticism on our part. That's the way it's supposed to be. Even people who say they believe in reincarnation do not perceive the full truth of it, for that would be too much for the human mind to handle.

Thomas Edison, the great inventor of the light bulb, believed that all atoms contain some form of consciousness. According to Kabbalah, Edison's view was not entirely accurate, for it implies that *atoms* and *consciousness* are two different entities. In other words, atoms do not *contain* consciousness. Atoms *are* consciousness. There is no such thing as mind over matter. Mind is matter.

Specifically, the *Zohar* says that consciousness consists of distinct forces of energy—the *Desire to Share* (proton), the *Desire to Receive* (electron), and the *Free Will* to choose (neutron). The fact that we are using different names to describe one singular idea does not mean that they are separate entities. All is one and one is all. When we sleep, this truth is evident to our souls.

The illusion we know as death occurs simply because we have accumulated a critical mass of negative consciousness that requires a very intense purification. The pain of death, and the pain experienced after death, purges the body of all negativity. This is not punishment, but its opposite—it provides the individual with another chance at paradise. He or she must be cleansed of the darkness accumulated over a lifetime before continuing to the next physical life on the path toward the ultimate reward of never-ending happiness and immortality.

When we finally transform into beings of unconditional sharing, we become immortal. How? Physics tells us that atoms are already immortal. Atoms don't decay. They are indestructible. What dies is the *form* that atoms create when they bond to produce molecules, which then bond with other molecules to produce cells, organs, and other tissues which ultimately create the body. Death is merely atoms letting go of each other, causing the demise of the molecule, and, in turn, the form the molecules create, which we know as the body. But individual atoms (consciousness) live on. It's a scientific fact—not that a kabbalist requires science to verify what he or she already knows.

The death of the form (the body) is a painful way to attain the transformation of mankind. We live and die—generation after generation—slowly evolving our consciousness through a path of pain and suffering. But there is an alternative. There always has been. There is a way to use sleep to battle pain, suffering, and the Angel of Death.

TASTE OF DEATH

Sleep is actually a taste of death. According to the *Zohar*, sleep is a taste of 1/60 of death. Therefore, each time we sleep, we have an opportunity to purify ourselves and correct our misdeeds of the previous day. When we sleep, we die a little, just for the time it takes our soul to leave the body and connect to the true and perfect reality. Through sleep, we have a tremendous opportunity to pay back all the debts we have created through the day, and to connect to the perfected world, completely recharging our soul. Now we're ready to begin a new day in a new life. Sleep truly is a merciful way to correct that which we damaged.

However, there is an even more powerful way to cleanse our souls, which also uses the power of the night to purify the body in a fashion that is not painful or filled with judgment. It's called *staying awake*! If that sounds like it contradicts everything I've said so far, please allow me to explain.

Chapter Three

The *Zohar* and the Power of Connection

THE POST-MIDNIGHT CONNECTION

We came here, to this physical existence, to fight, defeat, and ultimately transform the *Desire to Receive*. As we discussed, this desire is simply another term for an electron, and for the physical body. *Electron, Desire to Receive*, and *body* are all synonyms. When the body wants to sleep, and we fight it *for the sole purpose of connecting to the Light* that radiates from the Upper Worlds, this battle to stay awake purges the *Desire to Receive* and the force of death from our bodies.

Fighting sleep in order to connect to the Light weakens the body's grip on our lives. It raises our consciousness. And it tears away another layer of the death force from this world. For this reason, the great kabbalists of history used this exercise as a tool for connecting to the realm of perfection, to the dimension where there is no death.

The best opportunity for this connection occurs just after midnight every night. At that moment the cosmos literally opens up, and it is said that the Creator engages in the study of the *Zohar* with the greatest kabbalists of history in the Supernal Academy. Perhaps, if the Creator sees the value in a post-midnight connection to the *Zohar*, so should we. Should you choose to stay up and study after midnight, we have provided you with a section from the *Zohar* that you can study from and scan on page 103.

In the *Zohar*, in the section entitled "And It Came to Pass that at Midnight" *(Volume 9, Bo 5)*, it says the following in regard to the midnight hour:

> *Those who are awake rise; those who sleep awake. Worlds, prepare for Your Master. For your Master is going out to the Garden of Eden, which is His palace ... to delight with the Righteous.*

We have an opportunity to awake at midnight and touch the infinite because the Creator is going to take this opportunity to learn and delight in the great kabbalists.

The *Zohar* continues:

> *At the time that the Holy One, blessed be He, is revealed over the Garden, the whole Garden gathers, NAMELY ALL THE RIGHTEOUS IN THE GARDEN, but does not separate from Eden.... Springs emerge from this Eden ... to many ways and paths.... This Garden is called "The Bundle of Life," where the Righteous derive pleasure from the illumination of the World to Come. And at that time, the Holy One, blessed be He, reveals Himself to them.*

Not only does the *Zohar* reveal incredible secrets about what goes on in the spiritual realm when the clock strikes midnight, but the *Zohar* itself becomes the vehicle that allows us to attend this supernal gathering and capture Divine Energy and Light beyond all imagining. All we need to do is rise at midnight (or stay up until then) and study the *Zohar* with a friend or a teacher; we can also do this alone by simply allowing our eyes to scan the sacred texts in the comfort of our own homes. Visual scanning and meditating on the verses of the *Zohar* are powerful ways to send your soul soaring into the heavenly worlds, while at the same time battling and defeating the Angel of Death. The more tired you are, the more power you generate.

THE POWER OF THE *ZOHAR*

The *Zohar* is the direct expression and manifestation of the Light, which is simply a unique force of energy called *immortality*. This *Light of Immortality* is the Divine Force revealed on Mount Sinai by Moses. When speaking of the Revelation of Mount Sinai, all the religions of the world, including Islam and Christianity, are, in fact, referring to this special Force of Immortality that elevated every man, woman, and child on Earth at that time into a state of infinite joy and deathlessness.

The kabbalists refer to this Light as the *Or haGanuz* (The Hidden Light). They tell us that what really took place on Sinai was not the revelation of the Ten Commandments, but rather the connection of the Ten Dimensions (*Sefirot*). Our 1 Percent Reality (the world in which we live) hooked up with the 99 Percent Reality—the Tree of Life World of perfection, the Nine Hidden Dimensions that are the source of the Energy of the Creator.

Once these Ten Dimensions were aligned and connected as one, the energy of the Light was free to permeate our dimension. For this reason, the entire world—not just the Israelites—enjoyed the unspeakably blissful, infinitely pleasurable state of immortality while Moses was on Mount Sinai. At that moment, the only one dying was the Angel of Death. However, this utopian existence did not last. The Israelites built the golden calf, causing the entire world to lose Paradise. The Light vanished, to be stored inside the *Zohar*.

Think about that. When we scan or read the *Zohar* after midnight, while the body fights the force of sleep, the Light of Immortality removes the Angel of Death, and purges negativity and self-centeredness from our nature. As we fight to stay awake, the Angel of Death dies a little. As we battle sleep, the Light we are connecting to battles our ego, our ailments, and every bit of chaos in our life. This is unquestionably one of the most powerful tools we have, one that has remained hidden far too long from the world.

THE IRONY OF IT ALL

It is profoundly ironic that the greatest blow dealt to the Angel of Death, and all of his chaos, emerges from such a simple act as awakening after midnight to study spirituality from the *Zohar*, a source of Light. There's a good reason for this.

It would have been a simple matter for God to have created a giant stone tablet called the *Zohar*, placed it on top of a majestic mountain in Israel, and had it light up like a blazing sun every night at the stroke of midnight, so people all around the world could see and meditate on it in order to defeat the Angel of Death. But that would have been too easy. It would have been too obvious. The entire world would have embraced the *Zohar* without any real exercise of free will. We'd have earned nothing. We wouldn't have had to choose because there would have been no other choice. And in the process we wouldn't have had to exercise our humanity. We would have just reacted, like trained animals or sophisticated machines.

Instead, to give us the ability to become the cause of our own paradise, the Creator designed a world where the most powerful cosmic forces are concealed in the simplest of ordinary deeds. Where the greatest force of energy created is not in a nuclear reactor but inside a book. Where the greatest surge of spiritual power doesn't shoot down like flames from the heavens above but flows silently, invisibly, through ancient Aramaic letters on a page. Where the most profound transformation and hardcore spiritual work takes place not in a workout facility, or an army boot camp or an intense therapy session, but while we sleep, or battle to stay awake.

This completely misleading picture makes the truth almost impossible to believe. In fact, no logical person would ever believe it. This is why none of us are ever expected to just believe the truth. We have to experience it.

When you do, you will know it. Grasping the power of the *Zohar* and the power associated with staying awake past midnight is an *experience* of truth, not an intellectual, scientific, or rational understanding of truth. Yes, much of the time free will is a pain in the you-know-what! But it allows us to taste a tiny portion of the truth, even if the enormity and depth of it still has not shaken us to the bone. But if it's enough to stir us into action, to push us even a little bit toward connecting to the *Zohar* at the stroke of midnight, the exercise of free will has accomplished its mission. The results in your life (and the feeling in the depth of your being) will speak for themselves.

By the way, one way to detect the power of the *Zohar* is through the weight of the sleepiness that suddenly engulfs us during a midnight study session. When people gather at The Kabbalah Centers around the world during certain times of the year to engage in *Zohar*-learning after midnight, the feeling of exhaustion skyrockets and people are tempted to doze off immediately.

This is not a bad thing. And it's not that nothing exciting is happening. On the contrary, the Opponent, the Angel of Death, has been roused by the power emanating from the *Zohar,* and we find ourselves on the front lines of a battle. Isn't it brilliant that putting us to sleep, both figuratively and literally, is the most powerful of the Opponent's weapons?

Because the Opponent knows the importance of this battle, the *Zohar* provides a measure of protection for the person who rises to study. The *Zohar* also makes it clear that the benefits of this midnight reading are not limited to those who are actively learning from what they read. Everyone who tries will benefit.

> *He told me that when I wake up at midnight*
> *to study the Torah, my main objective should*
> *be the effort and not the knowledge.*
> —From The 134 Holy Sayings of Rav Ashlag

If we recognize the enemy, and lift ourselves out of our state of weariness, we are landing mighty blows against the Opponent, lessening the power of death in the world, and reducing the chances of physical wars.

Why? Every blow that we direct against our Opponent also weakens his influence in the lives of others. We are all interconnected. As we change, others change, because everyone is tied to the source of all hatred, conflict, and selfishness—the Opponent. By weakening him in ourselves, we weaken his cosmic influence, thereby weakening him in every single person on Earth. This is why we never, ever, try to change others. We only change ourselves—and *that* is what changes others. This insight is profound. Deep. Powerful.

Of course, if you were looking in from the outside, watching a group of people reading the *Zohar* in a Kabbalah Centre somewhere in the world, and you saw all the participants looking weary, you would never believe in a million years that you were witnessing the greatest battle in the universe. But that is precisely what you would be seeing. And the more we understand that, grasp it, and embrace it, the more powerful our victories will be. Our Opponent puts us to sleep by hiding this powerful truth, and he puts us to sleep physically during these *Zohar* sessions so that we do not gain an edge on the death force. Like I said, he is shrewd. Cunning. And he works tirelessly against us.

We have just discovered the power of battling the Opponent by remaining awake. Let us now examine some tools we can employ while entering into the state of sleep, as we do almost every night.

Chapter Four

Putting Sleep to Work for You

TAKING INVENTORY

Each night, before falling asleep, take inventory of your day, specifically identifying as much reactive, selfishly motivated behavior as possible. This is a powerful technology for discharging debts and releasing judgments we have aroused in the universe.

Humankind is not expected to defeat the consciousness of self-interest and reactivity. But we are expected to wage war against it, and recognize that this—and only this—is the root of our chaos, not some external enemy. Recognizing and admitting that the true battle lies within is unquestionably the most difficult of tasks. However, by investing time every night to identify the behaviors that work against us, we make this task manageable.

While we sleep, the dimension that we enter weakens and gradually tears away these negative influences. Once we identify the target, the Light battles even more effectively on our behalf. Rosh Hashanah and the month leading up to it—the Hebrew month of *Elul*—is a good time to review the negative actions of the year just past. However, our goal in taking inventory of our actions every night is to reach a place where the power and technologies associated with Rosh Hashanah won't even be necessary. If we do our work every night, we won't need to do any work at this cosmic event that launches another year.

FORGIVENESS

Just as important as taking inventory is the effort we put into forgiving, into letting go of all the animosity, revenge, hurt, and hostility that we are hanging on to. Releasing these completely through the act of forgiveness releases us from the clutches of the Opponent. Forgiveness pays.

There is a powerful Law of the Cosmos that works as follows: If we withhold judgment towards others, especially if the judgment is warranted, the universe must withhold equal judgment against us, even when we deserve the judgment. The Light of the Creator cannot and will not ever judge us. The Energy of the Creator is only merciful, compassionate, and kind. Therefore, the universe is wired up in a way that only we can judge ourselves. Here's how this happens. Our negative behavior creates *judgment boomerangs*. However, once they've been created they can only be launched by one force—the judgment we direct at others. That's the launching pad. So if we hold back our judgment, our own boomerangs will never get airborne and, therefore, will never return to strike us.

The software that runs the universe is designed to bring people who have committed negative acts similar to our own into our lives at every level—including business connections, friends, family, and strangers in the street. Now that we've met them, we have a choice: Judge them, or let it go. If we let it go, our own judgment boomerangs remain grounded. If we judge them, we launch judgments against ourselves. This is why we need to forgive everyone in our lives every night before we go to sleep.

Another reason to exercise forgiveness before we go to sleep is that the less emotional baggage we have to carry in our consciousness at bedtime, the higher our soul can ascend into the spiritual atmosphere.

Still another reason is that in our dreams we are all given glimpses of the future; we are sent messages. Sometimes the messages are false, and sometimes they are true. The clearer and more compassionate our consciousness is before drifting off to sleep, the more accurate the messages we receive.

Regarding the messages in our dreams, the *Zohar (Volume 15, Metzora 2:6)* states the following:

> *When the night falls and the gates are closed, a chasm in the great abyss is opened and many battalions of demons present in the world. Then, the Holy One, blessed be He, casts sleep upon all human beings in the world AND CASTS SLEEP even upon those who are awake, NAMELY THE RIGHTEOUS. AND THE SPIRITS go around the world and inform people of different matters IN THEIR DREAMS, part of which is false and part of which is truth. People are thus linked with them in their sleep.*

When there is judgment or vengeance in our hearts, we are open to hearing negative messages that mix truth with lies in order to give us a false impression of the future. Naturally, when that time is upon us and certain choices must be made, we make the wrong one because we've been deceived by our dreams. Do you ever smack yourself on the forehead and cry out "How could I have been so stupid?" Now you know. You dreamed it ahead of time, and you got it wrong.

Forgiving everyone and releasing judgment in our hearts prior to falling asleep ensures that we will receive truthful messages from positive forces (angels), as well as preventing judgment from entering into our lives.

THE JUDGING OF THE SOUL

Every night our soul enters into the higher reality of the Light and is judged for the deeds it performed that day. This judgment determines whether or not the soul is allowed to return to the body and continue toward its goal of transformation. Our soul also enters into the Upper Worlds to receive a recharge, a tune-up, because each day our negative behavior takes a terrible toll on the soul. Without sleep to renew us, the damage incurred to the soul by just a few days of self-centered behavior would cause immediate death. Instead of purifying the soul by dying in order to let the soul come back in a new body, we taste a little death—one-sixtieth—by sleeping. We discharge negative energy while we recharge the soul with positive energy.

The kabbalists tell us that each day, through our actions, we prepare a special bed for our soul. In other words, every day we make our own bed, and each and every night we must lie in it. Our soul either sleeps in a bed that dwells in Heaven, where it gets a pleasurable tune-up and battery charge, or it sleeps in a bed that dwells in Hell, which is the reason we have nightmares, where our soul is purified from the negativity we accumulated during the prior day. Where we sleep is up to us.

Most of our sleep disorders are an indication that we need to do more spiritual work. Spiritual work doesn't refer to meditation, prayer, song, or the practice of certain rites and rituals. Spiritual work refers to our interactions with others. Period. Spiritual behavior doesn't take place in a hermit's cave, or on a majestic mountaintop, or by a peaceful stream. It takes place in the subway. At work. In a crowd. In a business meeting. In the kitchen. In the car. It takes place during a heated argument. It occurs when chaos engulfs us. It happens at a busy intersection, when cars are honking at us, or people are shoving us.

The more difficult, hectic, and *real world* our situation is, the more opportunity it gives us for spiritual behavior. What is spiritual behavior? It means being proactive, regardless of the events around us, as opposed to being reactive. When we are reactive to anything—good or bad—we're just responding reflexively. Our true self—the proactive soul—is in a coma.

Being truly awake and alive is measured by the amount of proactive consciousness that governs our behavior. Ninety-nine percent of the world is in a constant state of reactivity, completely ignorant of the fact that the Opponent exists and has taken refuge in our rational mind. Thus we find ourselves trapped in a waking nightmare of pain, suffering, persecution, global warming, poverty, famine, and economic crisis. Not only is this comatose state the cause of all the ills of the world, it is also the cause of our sleep disorders.

The more reactive we are towards others, the greater chance that we'll suffer from a sleep disorder, since our soul is experiencing great discomfort. Why? It knows on a subconscious level that it's going to be spending a night in Hell, so it doesn't—and we don't—want to fall asleep. Or the body is fighting us because our Opponent does not want to be purified and removed from our nature during the night. So he keeps us awake, tossing and turning. We spend millions of dollars in research on the phenomenon of sleep, dreams, and sleep disorders, never realizing that our reactive, self-centered consciousness (and our refusal to accept and deal with it) is the ultimate cause.

Many years ago, a Kabbalah student kept waking up in the middle of the night and could not fall back asleep. Consequently, he went to work every day bleary-eyed and exhausted. Clearly, it was the Opponent who was disturbing his sleep, trying to prevent his soul from achieving its battery charge, so that he, the Opponent, could remain a powerful influence in the student's life.

One of our teachers told the student to open up the *Zohar* and meditate on it every time he woke up. He also instructed the student to thank the Opponent for waking him so that he could connect to the greatest source of spiritual energy in the cosmos. It was a shrewd piece of advice. So, what was the result after just a few nights of *Zohar* study? The Opponent stopped waking the student, who started sleeping peacefully through the night. His sleeping disorder was cured.

Taking inventory, offering forgiveness, connecting to the *Zohar* at midnight, sharing with others, and treating all people with dignity during the day—these are all tools that can and will cure any sleep disorder.

Here are a few more.

Chapter Five

The Bedtime *Shema* and the Power of One

Perhaps the most famous prayer connection associated with the path of the Torah and Kabbalah is the *Shema*, in which we declare the oneness of God. On a kabbalistic level, we are elevating ourselves out of this physical world of judgment and entering into the Tree of Life Reality, the 99 Percent World of perfection. This is not about declaring the oneness of God so much as it is about *achieving* oneness with the 99 Percent Reality. The words that compose the *Shema* are the technology for achieving the elevation and unification.

The *Zohar* tells us that the first five words of the *Shema* correspond to the five petals on a rose. Why a rose? We are the roses that sit among thorns, which represent the sharp and painful judgments of this world. When a rose opens up and emits a fragrance, it inspires passersby to enjoy its aroma and pluck the rose to share with a loved one. When we emit the fragrance of Light by sharing, life plucks us free from the thorns of judgment and we elevate to a higher level.

When we recite the Bedtime *Shema* at night, we are allowing our soul to rise out of this world into the waiting arms of the Creator. We literally surrender our body and place our life force—the soul—into the trust of the Creator. This ensures that we receive new spiritual power each night so we awake each morning healthy, strong, vibrant, aware, and committed to achieving everything we were meant to realize during this lifetime. To understand more about the Bedtime Shema connection and the rose, see the *Zohar, Volume 20 Pinchas 67, entitled "The Rose, Part Two."*

The last words we should recite before falling asleep should be the *Shema*. For those who cannot read Hebrew, scanning the *Shema* with the eyes will give you access and connection to its power.

PREVENTING NIGHTMARES —A QUICK CHEAT SHEET

Most nightmares serve a purpose. But some are simply the work of the Opponent. These particular nightmares serve no practical purpose other than to disrupt our sleep and make us fearful. For those of us who are experiencing one too many of these kinds of nightmares, there is a simple trick that we can use.

Simply recite the following phrase, which part of the Bedtime *Shema* on page 111.

← Reading from right to left

נַפְשִׁי אִוִּיתִךָ בַּלַּיְלָה מלה רוּחִי בְּקִרְבִּי שדי אֲשַׁחֲרֶךָ

ashacharecha vekir'bi ruchi af balayilah yiviticha nafshi

כִּי כַּאֲשֶׁר מִשְׁפָּטֶיךָ לָאָרֶץ צֶדֶק לָמְדוּ יֹשְׁבֵי

yoshvei lamdu tzedek la'aretz mishpatecha ka'asher ki

תֵבֵל ב"פ רי"ו:

tevel

WINDOWS IN TIME

The *Zohar* is very clear when it tells us that every night at midnight a window in the universe opens, and we can enter it to soak up Divine Energy through *Zohar* study. Sometimes, instead of just studying for a few minutes, a half hour, or an hour or two, students and kabbalists remain awake the entire night. The *Zohar* makes reference to this practice in the following verses, from Volume 15, *Metzora*:

> *When the north wind is awakened at midnight ... the Holy One, blessed be He, comes into the Garden of Eden to delight Himself with the righteous. An announcer comes out and proclaims, and all people awaken in their beds. Those who are awake stand by their beds to worship their Master. They learn Torah (Kabbalah) and praise the Holy One, blessed be He, until the morning comes.*

There are additional times throughout the year where the opening in the universe becomes more accessible. For instance, on the anniversaries of the deaths of the great kabbalistic sages, their souls come into our world to assist us with our elevation to the spiritual realm. Staying awake until sunrise for the purpose of connecting to these sages, and, in turn, to the Light of the Creator is a practice that has been carried out by kabbalists for some 2000 years.

Some of the great kabbalists whose death anniversaries (*passing anniversaries* is probably a more accurate term) are part of our technology include the following:

Rav Shimon bar Yochai: The passing of Rav Shimon took place on the 33rd day of the *Omer*, which is referred to as *Lag Ba'Omer*. When a righteous sage leaves the world, all the Light revealed in his or her lifetime is revealed on the day of his passing.

Think about this. Rav Shimon revealed the *Zohar*, which contains the Light that vanished on Mount Sinai as a result of the Israelites worshipping the golden calf. This means that the *Zohar* represents the energy of the Revelation of Mount Sinai, and therefore the power of immortality. Thanks to Rav Shimon, all of this Light is now available on the 33rd day of the *Omer*. Throughout history, students stay awake all night on *Lag Ba'Omer*, fighting sleep (death) and connecting to the force of immortality in its purest form.

Of course, the Opponent fears this night the most, which is why the world still largely remains asleep with regard to the power and opportunity available on this night. After all, who ever heard of *Lag Ba'Omer* outside of the ultra-religious community? It is now time to wake up to this truth, and to stay awake all night long during the 33rd day of the *Omer*, so that death will give way to immortality.

Rav Isaac Luria (the Ari): The anniversary of the Ari's passing occurs on the fifth day of the Hebrew month of *Av* (Leo). Rav Isaac Luria is the reincarnation of Rav Shimon bar Yochai, and therefore one of the greatest kabbalists in history. Make no mistake, without the Ari's revelations and writings deciphering the secrets of the *Zohar*, there would be no Kabbalah Centre and no book on Kabbalah accessible to more than a select few. The Ari deciphered the *Zohar* and unleashed its greatest secrets. Since the Ari is the reincarnation of Rav Shimon bar Yochai, not only does the anniversary of his passing awaken the full power of the Ari's insights into the *Zohar*, but it also allows us to tap into the power of Mount Sinai once again. Bear in mind that what activates this technology is our awareness of it. Now that you know, you can capture all the energy available on this powerful night.

Rachel the Matriarch: Rachel is considered to be the mother of all mankind, someone who sheds tears to this very day for the pain endured by her children. The date of her passing is on the 11th day of *Mar Cheshvan* (Scorpio). Staying up all night provides us with the power of her protection, and there is no stronger force on Earth than the protective love of a mother.

Joseph the Righteous: Joseph, according to Kabbalah, represents the spiritual dimension known as *Yesod*. This realm is the gateway through which all the Light of the Upper Nine Dimensions flows in order to reach our world. For this reason, we might think of Joseph as the banker of the cosmos. He holds all its riches, all its financial prosperity, as well as its natural resources, such as food and water. He is the source of sustenance on every level. So you can imagine the power we derive by staying awake, reading the *Zohar*, and battling sleep on the night of Joseph's passing. This occurs on the 27th day of *Tammuz* (Cancer).

HOLIDAY CONNECTION

A holiday connection is also an opportunity to connect to energy by battling sleep. For example, the holiday connection known as *Shavuot* is the day that Moses received the Revelation of Mount Sinai some 3400 years ago. As we've learned, the Revelation was the injection of spiritual energy, or Light, into our world, which banished death, at least for a time. This Light of Immortality shines again on *Shavuot*.

The ancient kabbalists tell us that if we stay awake all night on this occasion, we are absolutely guaranteed life until the following Rosh Hashanah. So, on each *Shavuot*, if we stay awake until sunrise, we restore a portion of the original Light of Immortality and ensure life—or as my father, Rav Berg, always says, "We receive *genuine* life insurance."

There are many more passing dates of great kabbalists that we use to make special connections throughout the year. For more information, go to www.kabbalah.com for a list of Kabbalah Centres around the world, and get in touch with the Centre nearest you.

Chapter Six

Why King David
Never Slept

King David never slept. Never. The most he rested each night was 20 minutes. Why? There are many profound reasons. But before I cover a few of the most important, I have to back up and give you some context.

The great patriarchs of the Bible, including Abraham, Isaac, Jacob, Joseph, Moses, Aaron, and King David, all correspond to parts of the spiritual communication system called *Sefirot*, through which the Light of the Creator flows to give existence to our world. These *Sefirot* are found in the subatomic quantum realm of our existence. All the so-called atoms, their subatomic particles—the proton, electron, and neutron—and their sub-subatomic particles, such as quarks, leptons, and gluons, are just manifestations of the spiritual energies of the *Sefirot*. The *Sefirot* are the interface between the Endless World—a realm of pure, infinite energy—and our physical reality.

The reason an atom contains three fundamental forces—protons, electrons, and neutrons—is they are simply the manifestations of the Three Columns of the

Sefirot, also known as the Tree of Life. The *Sefirot* are the mechanisms by which pure energy becomes physical matter, which is exactly what's happening in the quantum world, where subatomic particles gradually evolve from pure energy to create the illusion we know as our material world.

The ancient kabbalists explain that King David corresponds to the Tenth Dimension known as *Malchut*, which is our physical world. Like the moon, Malchut has no Light of its own. It is an empty Vessel. For this reason, King David came into this world with no life. To overcome this problem, Adam, the first man, bestowed upon David 70 years of his life. The *Zohar* reveals this secret in Volume 14, the chapter known as Vayechi:

> *It was decreed that Adam should live a thousand years, but seventy were removed from him to form King David's life and he gave them to him.*

King David lived on borrowed time (literally), and for this reason he refused to sleep at night so as not to have any connection to death, since sleep represents 1/60th of death. Whereas we may battle sleep (and thereby death) by staying awake at various times throughout the year, King David lived his entire life using this kabbalistic technology. The *Zohar* says:

> *Rav Yehuda was then saying to Rav Yosi: We have learned that King David slept like a horse and had little sleep. If this is true, how did he wake up at midnight? The portion OF SIXTY BREATHS OF A HORSE'S SLEEP is very brief, so he would have awakened before even a third of the night was over. He replied: When night fell, he used to sit with the princes of his house to execute justice and study the Torah, WHICH MEANS, THAT HE DID NOT GO TO SLEEP WHEN NIGHT FELL, BUT CLOSER TO MIDNIGHT. He then slept until midnight, when he woke and rose to*

worship his Master with songs and hymns. The man interposed and asked: Is this what you think? This is the secret of the matter: King David is alive and exists forever and ever. King David was careful to avoid a foretaste of death; and because sleep is a sixtieth part of death, King David, whose domain is the Living, slept only sixty breaths. For up to sixty breaths less one, it is living; from then on, man tastes death and the side of the impure spirit reigns over him. King David guarded himself from tasting death, lest the side of the impure spirit obtain control over him. For sixty breaths minus one are the Secret of Supernal Life. The first sixty breaths are the Supernal sixty breaths, whose secret is that life depends on them. From then downward, it is the secret of death. Therefore King David would measure the night UNTIL MIDNIGHT, so as to remain alive, lest the foretaste of death dominate him. At midnight, David would be in his domain, IN HIS GRADE, WHICH IS LIFE AND EXISTENCE, BY WAKING UP AND UTTERING CHANTS AND HYMNS. For when midnight stirred and the Holy Crown, THE NUKVA, was awakened, David did not wish to be found connected to another domain, the domain of death. When midnight comes Supernal Holiness is awakened, but man is asleep in his bed and does not awaken to regard the glory of his Master; he becomes attached to the secret of death and cleaves to another domain, TO THE OTHER SIDE. King David therefore always woke at midnight, careful of the glory of his Master, alive before the Living One, and he would never sleep long enough to taste death. Thus, he slept like the sixty breaths of a horse—sixty breaths LESS ONE.

—The Zohar, Vayigash 5:34-39

It is known that the Messiah (world peace and immortality) is a descendent of King David. He is known as "Messiah, the son of David." From David's life we can learn how to hasten the arrival of the Messiah and the state of immortality it will create. By following King David's example of not sleeping in order to connect to the Light, we accelerate the arrival of the Messiah. By injecting the thought of King David into our consciousness while battling sleep, we actually expedite the transformation of the world. Consciousness, awareness, and knowledge of what we want are the most powerful accelerators for achieving this goal of all goals. This is why King David came into the world. Simply by directing our consciousness toward him when waging war against sleep, we can tap into a source of tremendous power and energy.

Because King David did not have the opportunity to pay back his karmic debts through sleep, as we do, he was forced to endure all the pain of the world in his waking state. He had spiritual surgery without any anesthesia, and he did it for us. Fortunately, he had the strength to shoulder an enormous and disproportionate amount of responsibility and pain so that the rest of the world, and all future generations, would not have to do so. But to take advantage of this situation, we must be aware of it.

When life is too painful, when the pain of others and ills of the world are too much for us, the universe helps us transform in our sleep. David did not have that luxury. He met the ills of the world head-on. When people see too much suffering, they often lose faith in God. They cannot see the big picture, the Cause and Effect relationship that brought about the intense suffering. David was a man of such power that he was able to see, in his waking state, the suffering of life, and experience it for himself, without losing certainty in the existence of the Creator.

Sleep was given to mankind as a gift so that we could deal with a lot of these pressures in a state of anesthesia. In addition to using sleep each night to help us achieve the final goal, we should also follow the example of King David and open our eyes a little wider during the waking state. See and feel the pain of the world, if only just a little bit. If everyone who reads this book is willing to shoulder just a little bit more pain, the load will be lighter for everyone else. And therein lies the paradox. If we are willing to take on more pain, and enough people do it, we won't have to experience as much pain individually to achieve the final goal.

RESURRECTION OF THE DEAD

When talking about immortality people often wonder about ideas such as the Resurrection of the Dead, and who will be included in a world of immortality.

Make no mistake: Death is merely an illusion, the disappearance of a certain physical form; the soul, which is immortal, will return in a new configuration of atoms and molecules to finish its transformation.

There are those beings throughout history who have completed their transformations and therefore exist in a different reality until such time as our physical world completes its final correction. In the same way that certain frequencies or wavelengths of light are invisible to the naked eye but are still all around us, the frequencies of these transformed souls are here with us, right now.

The Resurrection of the Dead is not to be taken literally. In fact, Kabbalah teaches us to see the encoded messages in most of what we read in the Torah, or the Bible. If we are truly awake in our sleep state, and truly asleep in what we think of as our daily existence, perhaps the term *Resurrection of the Dead* refers to what will happen to us! When we are truly awake we will begin to see those who have already passed on. When our eyes open to the deeper truth that death is not real, we will find that everyone is still here.

As the *Desire to Receive* is eradicated from our consciousness, other frequencies of reality suddenly appear, and we wake up to realms more glorious, more beautiful, simple, and blissful than we could have ever imagined. Everyone who ever lived is there with us. All paradoxes are resolved, and we know with utter certainty that this life was a dream designed by the Creator to give us the ability to create our final world through our own efforts.

And that is when we realize the ultimate truth: There is something *better* than unending happiness. What could possibly be better than infinite happiness? It is the ability to be the Cause and creators of our own infinite, unending happiness.

This is the greatest gift of the Creator. Before going to sleep every night, take a moment to savor it; your appreciation will hasten the arrival of immortality, and immortality will all unfold with the pleasantness of a delightful dream.

Sleep well!

Part Two

Tools

The Bedtime *Shema*

When the sun has set and the stars begin to appear in the heavens, part of our soul leaves us. Even if we remain awake, the soul departs, which is the reason why we feel progressively more tired as the night unfolds. The more negative we are, the more drained we feel when our soul leaves.

There is an actual force that induces us to sleep each night to allow the soul to vacate the body. We recite the *Shema* to attach an umbilical cord to our soul so that it will return and fill the space that it left behind.

The *Shema* injects the nurturing Light of the Creator into the 248 bone segments and joints and 365 sinews of a man's body and the 252 bone segments, joints and the 365 sinews of a woman's body. To be able to receive this Light, we must have absolute certainty in the power of this prayer. When reciting or scanning the *Shema*, what we look at and think we want, as well as what we say we want, should be what our heart and soul *truly* desire—to know that the Light is filling every part of our body.

If someone harbors any ill feeling toward another person as he goes to sleep, this animosity will prevent both souls from elevating to the Upper Worlds during the night. In this prayer, we ask forgiveness from those people we've hurt. It is important to take a moment and reflect on our day and search for any negativity that we may have caused to others or that others may have caused us. We need to acknowledge that we must seek forgiveness for every injury we have caused, whether intentional or accidental, through words or through physical activity, in this lifetime or in a past lifetime.

Before we begin the *Shema*, we recite *LeShem Yichud*, which acts like a spark plug, activating the next series of prayers and actions. All kabbalistic meditations are read or scanned from right to left.

LESHEM YICHUD

לְשֵׁם יִחוּד קוּדְשָׁא בְּרִיךְ הוּא וּשְׁכִינְתֵּיהּ בִּדְחִילוּ

bid'chilu ush'chinteh hu berich kudsha yichud l'shem

וּרְחִימוּ, וּרְחִימוּ וּדְחִילוּ, לְיַחֲדָא שֵׁם יוֹ״ד קֵי בְּוָא״ו

beVav Kei Yud shem leyachda ud'chilu ur'chimu ur'chimu

קֵי בְּיִחוּדָא שְׁלִים בְּשֵׁם כָּל יְלִי יִשְׂרָאֵל, הֲרֵינִי מְקַבֵּל

mekabel hareni Israel kol b'shem sh'lim b'yichuda Kei

עָלַי אֱלָהוּתוֹ יִתְבָּרֵךְ וְאַהֲבָתוֹ וְיִרְאָתוֹ, וַהֲרֵינִי יָרֵא

yare vehareni veyirato ve'ahavat yitbarach Elahuto alai

מִמֶּנוּ בְּגִין דְּאִיהוּ רַב וְשַׁלִּיט עַל כּוּלָא, וְכוּלָא

vechula kula al veshalit rav dehihu begin mimenu

קַמֵיהּ כְּלָא, וַהֲרֵינִי מַמְלִיכוּ עַל כָּל יְלִי אֵבֶר וְאֵבֶר

ve'ever ever kol al mamlicho vehareni kela kamei

וְגִיד וְגִיד מֵרַמַ״ח אברהם אֵבָרִים וְשַׁסַ״ה גִּידִים שֶׁל

shel gidim veshasa evarim meramach vagid vegid

גּוּפִי וְנַפְשִׁי רוּחִי וְנִשְׁמָתִי מַלְכוּת גְּמוּרָה וּשְׁלֵמָה,

ushlemah gemurah malchut venishmati ruchi venafshi gufi

וַהֲרֵינִי עֶבֶד לְהַשֵׁיְ״ת, וְהוּא בְּרַחֲמָיו יְזַכֵּנִי לְעָבְדוֹ

le'avdo yezakeni berachamav vehu lehasheyi"t eved vahareni

בְּלֵבָב בוכו שָׁלֵם וְנֶפֶשׁ וַחֲפֵצָה אָמֵן כֵּן יְהִי רָצוֹן מהש״ע:

ratzon yehi ken amen chafetzah venefesh shalem b'levav

RIBONO SHEL OLAM

רִבּוֹנוֹ שֶׁל עוֹלָם הֲרֵינִי מוֹחֵל וְסוֹלֵחַ לְכָל מִי י'יִ
mi lechol vesole'ach mochel hareni olam shel ribono

שֶׁהִכְעִיס וְהִקְנִיט אוֹתִי אוֹ שֶׁחָטָא כְּנֶגְדִי. בֵּין בְּגוּפִי
begufi bein kenegdi shechata o oti vehik'nit shehich'is

בֵּין בְּמָמוֹנִי בֵּין בִּכְבוֹדִי בֵּין בְּכָל לכב אֲשֶׁר לִי .בֵּין
bein li asher bechol bein bichvodi bein bemamoni bein

בְּאוֹנֶס בֵּין בְּרָצוֹן מהע בֵּין בְּשׁוֹגֵג בֵּין בְּמֵזִיד בֵּין
bein bemezid bein beshogeg bei beratzon bein be'ones

בְּדִבּוּר בֵּין בְּמַעֲשֶׂה. בֵּין בְּגִלְגּוּל זֶה בֵּין בְּגִלְגּוּל
begilgul bein zeh begilgul bein bema'aseh bein bedibur

אַחֵר לְכָל בַּר יִשְׂרָאֵל וְלֹא יֵעָנֵשׁ שׁוּם אָדָם בְּסִבָּתִי.
besibati adam shum ye'anesh velo Israel bar lechol acher

יְהִי רָצוֹן מהע מִלְּפָנֶיךָ יְהֹוָהאלהיהאהדונהי אֱלֹהַי דמב וֵאלֹהֵי לכב
ve'Eloihei Elohai Adonai mil'fanecha ratzon yehi

אֲבוֹתַי שֶׁלֹּא אֶחֱטָא עוֹד. וּמַה שֶׁחָטָאתִי לְפָנֶיךָ
lefanecha shecha'tati umah od echeta shelo avotai

מְחוֹק בְּרַחֲמֶיךָ הָרַבִּים אֲבָל לֹא עַל יְדֵי יִסּוּרִין
yisurin yedei al lo aval harabim berachamech mechok

וְזוֹלְאִים רָעִים: יִהְיוּ לְרָצוֹן מהש אִמְרֵי פִי וְהֶגְיוֹן

veheg'yon   fi   im'rei   ldratzon   yihyu   ra'im   vdchola'im

לִבִּי לְפָנֶיךָ יְהֹוָאדְנִי צוּרִי וְגֹאֲלִי:

vdgo'ali   tzuri   Adonai   ldfanecha   libi

HAMAPIL

Hamapil ensures that our soul departs safely from our sleeping body and returns to our body when we awake. It is the lifeline between the body and the soul.

If we go to sleep before midnight, we start with *"Baruch Atah Adonai…"*

If we go to sleep after midnight, we start with *"Baruch…"* skipping the words in parentheses and continue with *"Hamapil chev'lei…"*

בָּרוּךְ (אַתָּה יְהֹוָאדְנִי אֱלֹהֵינוּ ילה מֶלֶךְ הָעוֹלָם)

(ha'olam   melech   Eloheinu   Adonai   atah) baruch

הַמַּפִּיל וְבְלֵי שֵׁנָה עַל עֵינַי וּתְנוּמָה עַל עַפְעַפָּי

af'apai   al   ut'mumah   einai   al   sheina   chev'lei   hamapil

וּמֵאִיר לְאִישׁוֹן בַּת עָיִן: יְהִי רָצוֹן מהש מִלְפָנֶיךָ

milefanecha   ratzon   yehi   ayin   bat   le'ishon   ume'ir

יְהֹוָאדְנִי אֱלֹהַי רמב וֵאלֹהֵי לכב אֲבוֹתַי שֶׁתַּשְׁכִּיבֵנִי

shetashkiveni   avotai   ve'Elohei   Elohai   Adonai

לְשָׁלוֹם וְתַעֲמִידֵנִי לְחַיִּים טוֹבִים וּלְשָׁלוֹם וְתֶן חֶלְקִי

chelki veten uleshalom tovim lechaim v'ta'amideni leshalom

בְּתוֹרָתֶךָ וְתַרְגִּילֵנִי לִדְבַר רֹאָה מִצְוָה וְאַל תַּרְגִּילֵנִי

tar'gileni ve'al mitzvah lid'var vetar'gileni betoratecha

לִדְבַר רֹאָה עֲבֵרָה. וְאַל תְּבִיאֵנִי לִידֵי וְלֹא חֵטְא וְלֹא לִידֵי

lidei velo chet lidei tevi'eni ve'al averah lid'var

נִסָּיוֹן וְלֹא לִידֵי בִזָּיוֹן. וְיִשְׁלוֹט בִּי יֵצֶר הַטּוֹב וְהֵ וְאַל

ve'al hatov yetzer bi veyishlot vizayon lidei velo nisa'yon

יִשְׁלוֹט בִּי יֵצֶר הָרָע. וְתַצִּילֵנִי מִיֵּצֶר הָרָע וּמֵחֳלָאִים

umechola'im hara miyetzer vetatzileni hara yetzer bi yishlot

רָעִים וְאַל יַבְהִילוּנִי וְחֲלוֹמוֹת רָעִים וְהִרְהוּרִים רָעִים

ra'im vehirhurim ra'im chalomot yav'hiluni ve'al ra'im

וּתְהֵא מִטָּתִי שְׁלֵמָה לְפָנֶיךָ וְהָאֵר עֵינַי פֶּן אִישַׁן הַמָּוֶת.

hamavet ishan pen einai veha'er lefanecha shelemah mitati ute'he

בָּרוּךְ אַתָּה יְהֹוָה־אֲדֹנָי־אֲהַדֹּנֵים הַמֵּאִיר לָעוֹלָם כֻּלּוֹ בִּכְבוֹדוֹ:

bich'vodo kulo la'olam hameir Adonai atah baruch

THE SHEMA

Before we start the *Shema*, it's important to think about the concept of loving our neighbors as we love ourselves. Even more powerful, is to meditate on someone else who needs healing, because by thinking of others we can achieve more healing for ourselves.

The first verse of the *Shema* channels the energy of the Upper Worlds. The second verse expresses that energy in our physical world. There are a total of 248 words in this prayer which transmit healing energy to the 248 parts of the human body. The first two verses have 12 words. The first section of the *Shema* is built of 42 words signifying the 42-letter Name of God, the *Ana Beko'ach*. The second section is composed of 72 words that connect to the 72 Names of God. The third section contains 50 words, which link us to the 50 Gates of Light that are contained in the *Sefirah* known as *Binah*. This link helps us rise above the 50 gates of negativity.

The last part of the *Shema* has 72 words; however, because this is a different combination of letters, this part of the prayer provides a different connection to the 72 names of God.

We cover our eyes with our right hand while saying the first two verses: *Shema Yisrael* and *Baruch Shem Kevod*.

עַ יִשְׂרָאֵל שְׁמַע
Israel Shema

יְהֹוָה אֱלֹהֵינוּ ילה
Eloheinu Adonai

אֶחָד יְהֹוָה
Echad Adonai

בְּלֹחֵע בָּרוּךְ שֵׁם כְּבוֹד מַלְכוּתוֹ, לְעוֹלָם וָעֶד:
(Whisper:) Va'ed le'olam malchuto kevod shem baruch

ג

וְאָהַבְתָּ אֵת יְהֹוָה(אדניאהדונהי) אֱלֹהֶיךָ בְּכָל לְבָבְךָ וּבְכָל

uvechol   lvavcha   bechol   Elohecha   Adonai   et   vahavta

נַפְשְׁךָ וּבְכָל מְאֹדֶךָ: וְהָיוּ הַדְּבָרִים הָאֵלֶּה אֲשֶׁר

asher   ha'eleh   hadvarim   v'hayu   m'odecha   uv'chol   nafshecha

אָנֹכִי מְצַוְּךָ הַיּוֹם עַל לְבָבֶךָ: וְשִׁנַּנְתָּם לְבָנֶיךָ

levanecha   vshinantam   levavecha   al   hayom   metzavcha   anochi

וְדִבַּרְתָּ בָּם בְּשִׁבְתְּךָ בְּבֵיתֶךָ וּבְלֶכְתְּךָ בַדֶּרֶךְ

vaderech   uv'lech'techa   beveitecha   beshivtcha   bam   ve'adibarta

וּבְשָׁכְבְּךָ וּבְקוּמֶךָ: וּקְשַׁרְתָּם לְאוֹת עַל יָדֶךָ

yadecha   al   le'ot   ukshartam   uv'kumecha   uv'shachvcha

וְהָיוּ לְטֹטָפֹת בֵּין עֵינֶיךָ: וּכְתַבְתָּם עַל מְזוּזוֹת

mezuzot   al   uch'tavtam   einecha   bein   letotafot   vehayu

בֵּיתֶךָ וּבִשְׁעָרֶיךָ:

uvish'arecha   beitecha

וְהָיָה יהה אִם יורך שָׁמֹעַ תִּשְׁמְעוּ אֶל מִצְוֹתַי אֲשֶׁר אָנֹכִי אייע

anochi asher mitzvotai el tish'm'u shamo'a im vehayah

מְצַוֶּה אֶתְכֶם הַיּוֹם נגד, זן לְאַהֲבָה אֶת יְהֹוָאדנילאהדונהי

Adonai et le'ahavah hayom et'chem metzaveh

אֱלֹהֵיכֶם ילה וּלְעָבְדוֹ בְּכָל לבב לְבַבְכֶם וּבְכָל לבב

uvechol levavchem bechol ul'avdo Eloheichem

w

נַפְשְׁכֶם: וְנָתַתִּי מְטַר אַרְצְכֶם בְּעִתּוֹ יוֹרֶה וּמַלְקוֹשׁ

umalkosh yore beito artzechem metar venatati nafshechem

וְאָסַפְתָּ דְגָנֶךָ וְתִירֹשְׁךָ וְיִצְהָרֶךָ: וְנָתַתִּי עֵשֶׂב

esev venatati veyitzharecha vetirosh'cha deganecha ve'asafta

בְּשָׂדְךָ לִבְהֶמְתֶּךָ וְאָכַלְתָּ וְשָׂבָעְתָּ: הִשָּׁמְרוּ לָכֶם

lachem hishamru vesava'ata ve'achalta liv'hem'techa besad'cha

פֶּן יִפְתֶּה לְבַבְכֶם וְסַרְתֶּם וַעֲבַדְתֶּם אֱלֹהִים ילה

Elohim va'avad'tem vesar'tem levav'chem yifteh pen

אֲחֵרִים וְהִשְׁתַּחֲוִיתֶם לָהֶם:

lahem vehish'tachavitem acherim

וְחָרָה (pause) אַף יְהֹוָאדנילאהדונהי בָּכֶם וְעָצַר אֶת

et ve'atzar bachem Adonai af vecharah

הַשָּׁמַיִם וְלֹא יִהְיֶה ⁓ מָטָר וְהָאֲדָמָה לֹא תִתֵּן ב"פ כהת
titen lo veha'adamah matar yih'yeh ve'lo ha'shama'yim

אֶת יְבוּלָהּ וַאֲבַדְתֶּם מְהֵרָה מֵעַל עלה הָאָרֶץ הַטֹּבָה
hatovah ha'aretz meal em'herah va'avadetem ey'vulah et

אֲשֶׁר יְהֹוָה אלהיאהדונהי נֹתֵן אבג יתץ, ושד לָכֶם:
lachem noten Adonai asher

ו

וְשַׂמְתֶּם אֶת דְּבָרַי ראה אֵלֶּה עַל לְבַבְכֶם וְעַל
ve'al levav'chem al eleh devarai et vesam'tem

נַפְשְׁכֶם וּקְשַׁרְתֶּם אֹתָם לְאוֹת עַל יֶדְכֶם וְהָיוּ
ve'hayu yed'chem al le'ot otam ukshar'tem naf'shechem

לְטוֹטָפֹת בֵּין עֵינֵיכֶם: וְלִמַּדְתֶּם אֹתָם אֶת בְּנֵיכֶם
beneichem et otam ve'limad'tem eineichem bein l'totafot

לְדַבֵּר ראה בָּם בְּשִׁבְתְּךָ בְּבֵיתֶךָ ב"פ ראה וּבְלֶכְתְּךָ
uv'lech'techa beveitecha beshiv'techa bam ledaber

בַדֶּרֶךְ ב"פ יב"ק וּבְשָׁכְבְּךָ וּבְקוּמֶךָ: וּכְתַבְתָּם עַל
al uch'tavtam uv'kumecha uv'shachbe'cha vaderech

מְזוּזוֹת בֵּיתֶךָ ב"פ ראה וּבִשְׁעָרֶיךָ: לְמַעַן יִרְבּוּ יְמֵיכֶם
yemeichem yir'bu lema'an uvish'arecha beitecha mezuzot

וִימֵי בְנֵיכֶם עַל הָאֲדָמָה אֲשֶׁר נִשְׁבַּע יְהֹוָה

vi'mei veneichem al ha'adamah asher nish'ba Adonai

לַאֲבֹתֵיכֶם לָתֵת לָהֶם כִּימֵי הַשָּׁמַיִם עַל הָאָרֶץ:

la'avoteichem latet lahem ki'mei hashama'yim al ha'aretz

ה

וַיֹּאמֶר יְהֹוָה אֶל מֹשֶׁה לֵּאמֹר: דַבֵּר אֶל

Adonai vayomer el Moshe le'emor daber el

בְּנֵי יִשְׂרָאֵל וְאָמַרְתָּ אֲלֵהֶם וְעָשׂוּ לָהֶם צִיצִת עַל

benei Israel ve'amarta aleihem ve'asu lahem tzizit al

כַּנְפֵי בִגְדֵיהֶם לְדֹרֹתָם וְנָתְנוּ עַל צִיצִת הַכָּנָף פְּתִיל

kan'fei vigdeihem le'dorotam venatnu al tzizit hakanaf petil

תְּכֵלֶת: וְהָיָה יְהֹוָה לָכֶם לְצִיצִת וּרְאִיתֶם אֹתוֹ וּזְכַרְתֶּם

techelet vehayah letzitzit lachem ur'item oto uz'char'tem

אֶת כָּל יְהֹוָה מִצְוֹת יְהֹוָה וַעֲשִׂיתֶם אֹתָם וְלֹא תָתוּרוּ

et kol mitzvot Adonai va'asitem otam velo taturu

אַחֲרֵי לְבַבְכֶם וְאַחֲרֵי עֵינֵיכֶם אֲשֶׁר אַתֶּם זֹנִים

Acharei levav'chem ve'acharei eineichem asher atem zonim

אַחֲרֵיהֶם: לְמַעַן תִּזְכְּרוּ וַעֲשִׂיתֶם אֶת כָּל יְהֹוָה מִצְוֹתָי

achareihem lema'an tiz'keru va'asitem et kol mitzvotai

וִהְיִתֶם קְדֹשִׁים לֵאלֹהֵיכֶם יל׳ה: אֲנִי אֲנִי יְהֹוָּהֵוּוּ
vihitem kedoshim le'eloheichem ani ani Adonai

אֱלֹהֵיכֶם אֲשֶׁר הוֹצֵאתִי אֶתְכֶם מֵאֶרֶץ מִצֵּר מִצְרַיִם
Eloheichem asher hotzeti et'chem me'eretz Mitzrayim

לִהְיוֹת לָכֶם לֵאלֹהִים יל׳ה: אֲנִי יְהֹוָּהֵוּוּ
lih'yot lachem le'Elohim ani Adonai

אֱלֹהֵיכֶם יל׳ה:
Eloheichem

אֱמֶת
Emet

יְהֹוָּהֵוּוּ אֱלֹהֵיכֶם יל׳ה: אֱמֶת
Adonai Eloheichem emet

YA'ALZU

Every act of wrongdoing we commit produces negative angels that surround us each and every day. These negative entities are often the unseen cause of all those things, large and small, that go wrong in our lives. These verses help remove those negative angels and their destructive influence and we recite them three times:

יַעְלְזוּ חֲסִידִים בְּכָבוֹד יְרַנְּנוּ עַל מִשְׁכְּבוֹתָם:
ya'alzu chasidim bechavod yeran'nu al mish'kevotam

רוֹמְמוֹת אֵל בִּגְרוֹנָם וְחֶרֶב רי׳ו פִּיפִיּוֹת בְּיָדָם:
romemot el big'ronam vecherev pifyot beyadam

HINEH MITATO

The kabbalists teach there is an element of death (1/60th), that takes place when we sleep because a part of the soul departs the body. It's important to question ourselves as if this night is our last night and ask: "Did I do enough spiritual change in my life today? Am I happy that this is my last day?"

These next verses contain 20 words and when we recite them three times (20 x 3 = 60), they protect us against the energy of death that occurs when we sleep.

הִנֵּה מִטָּתוֹ שֶׁלִּשְׁלֹמֹה שִׁשִּׁים גִּבֹּרִים סָבִיב לָהּ

la   saviv   giborim   shishim   shelish'lomo   mitato   hineh

מִגִּבֹּרֵי יִשְׂרָאֵל: כֻּלָּם אֲחֻזֵי חֶרֶב מְלֻמְּדֵי מִלְחָמָה

milchamah   melum'dei   cherev   achuzei   kulam   Israel   migiborei

אִישׁ חַרְבּוֹ רַיַי עַל יְרֵכוֹ מִפַּחַד בַּלֵּילוֹת:

baleilot   mipachad   yerecho   al   charbo   ish

BLESSING OF THE *KOHENIM*

Kohenim (priests) have the innate power to channel the forces of healing from the Upper Worlds into our physical reality. By reciting these verses, we receive a tremendous force of healing.

בְּרֶכְךָ יְהוָֹאלהיםאהדונהי וְיִשְׁמְרֶךָ: לּ   Right Column

veyish'merecha   Adonai   yevarechecha

אֵר יְהוָֹאלהיםאהדונהי פָּנָיו אֵלֶיךָ וִיחֻנֶּךָּ מנר: לּ   L eft Column

vichunecha   eleicha   panav   Adonai   ya'er

שָּׂא יְהוָֹאלהיםאהדונהי פָּנָיו אֵלֶיךָ וְיָשֵׂם לְךָ לּ   Central Column

Echa   veyasem   eilecha   panav   Adonai   yisa

שָׁלוֹם:

shalom

YOSHEV BESETER

This Psalm contains 60 words, giving us another opportunity to receive protection from death.

יֹשֵׁב בְּסֵתֶר ב״פ מצר עֶלְיוֹן בְּצֵל שַׁדַּי יִתְלוֹנָן: אֹמַר

omar yit'lonan Shadai betzel el'yon beseter yoshev

לַיהֹוָהדוהי־אהדונהי מַחְסִי וּמְצוּדָתִי אֱלֹהַי דמב אֶבְטַח בּוֹ: כִּי

ki bo evtach Elohai um'tzudati mach'si la'Adonai

הוּא יַצִּילְךָ מִפַּח יָקוּשׁ מִדֶּבֶר הַוּוֹת: בְּאֶבְרָתוֹ

be'evrato havot midever yakush mipach yatzil'cha hu

יָסֶךְ לָךְ וְתַחַת כְּנָפָיו תֶּחְסֶה צִנָּה וְסֹחֵרָה אֲמִתּוֹ:

amito vesocherah tzinah tech'se kenafav vetachat lach yasech

לֹא תִירָא מִפַּחַד לָיְלָה מֵחֵץ יָעוּף יוֹמָם:

yomam ya'uf mechetz la'yilah mipachad tira lo

מִדֶּבֶר בָּאֹפֶל יַהֲלֹךְ מִקֶּטֶב יָשׁוּד צָהֳרָיִם: יִפֹּל

yipol tzahara'yim yashud miketev yahaloch ba'ofel midever

מִצִּדְּךָ אֶלֶף וּרְבָבָה מִימִינֶךָ אֵלֶיךָ לֹא יִגָּשׁ: רַק

rak yigash lo eleicha miyeminecha urvavah elef mitzidecha

בְּעֵינֶיךָ תַבִּיט וְשִׁלֻּמַת רְשָׁעִים תִּרְאֶה ראה: כִּי

ki tir'eh resha'im veshilumat tabit beineicha

אַתָּה יְהֹוָהדוהי־אהדונהי מַחְסִי.

mach'si Adonai atah

VIDU'I

The *Vidu'i* is to be said only on weekdays, not on Shabbat and holidays. All our wrongful actions leave a residue in our body. These connections cleanse all these negative remnants.

אָנָּא יְהֹוָהאלי־אהדונהי אֱלֹהֵינוּ ילה וֵאלֹהֵי לכב אֲבוֹתֵינוּ. תָּבֹא

tavo   avoteinu   ve'Elohei   Eloheinu   Adonai   ana

לְפָנֶיךָ תְּפִלָּתֵנוּ וְאַל תִּתְעַלַּם מַלְכֵּנוּ מִתְּחִנָּתֵנוּ. שֶׁאֵין

she'ein   mit'chinatenu   mal'kenu   tit'alam   ve'al   tefilatenu   lefanecha

אֲנוּ עַזֵּי פָנִים וּקְשֵׁי עֹרֶף לוֹמַר לְפָנֶיךָ יְהֹוָהאלי־אהדונהי

Adonai   lefanecha   lomar   oref   uk'shei   panim   azei   anachnu

אֱלֹהֵינוּ ילה וֵאלֹהֵי לכב אֲבוֹתֵינוּ צַדִּיקִים אֲנַחְנוּ וְלֹא

velo   anachnu   tzadikim   avoteinu   ve'Eloheinu   Eloheinu

וְחָטָאנוּ. אֲבָל וְחָטָאנוּ. עָוִינוּ. פָּשַׁעְנוּ. אֲנַחְנוּ

anachnu   pasha'nu   avinu   chatanu   aval   chatanu

וַאֲבוֹתֵינוּ וְאַנְשֵׁי בֵיתֵנוּ:

beitenu   ve'an'shei   va'avoteinu

אָ שַׁמְנוּ. בָּ גַדְנוּ. גָּ זַלְנוּ. דִּ בַּרְנוּ דוֹפִי וְלָשׁוֹן הָרָע.

ha'rah   velashon   dofi   dibar'nu   gazal'nu   bagad'nu   asham'nu

הֶ עֱוִינוּ. וְ הִרְשַׁעְנוּ. זַ דְנוּ. חָ מַסְנוּ. טָ פַלְנוּ שֶׁקֶר וּמִרְמָה.

umir'mah   sheker   tafal'nu   chamas'nu   zad'nu   vehir'sha'nu   he'evinu

לָ עָצֵנוּ עֵצוֹת רָעוֹת. כִּזַּבְנוּ. כָּעַסְנוּ. כָ צְנוּ. לַ צְנוּ. מָ רַדְנוּ.

marad'nu latz'nu ka'as'nu kizav'nu ra'ot etzot ya'atz'nu

מָרִינוּ דְבָרֶיךָ. נָ אַצְנוּ. נִאַפְנוּ. סָ רַרְנוּ. עָ וִינוּ. פָ שַׁעְנוּ.

pasha'anu avinu sarar'nu niaf'nu niatz'nu devarecha marinu

פָּגַמְנוּ. צָ רַרְנוּ. צִעַרְנוּ אָב וָאֵם. קִ שִׁינוּ עֹרֶף.

oref kishinu va'em av tzi'ar'nu tzarar'nu pagam'nu

רָ שַׁעְנוּ. שִׁ חַתְנוּ. תִּ עַבְנוּ. תָּעִינוּ. וְתִעֲתַּעְנוּ וְסַרְנוּ

vesar'nu vetia'ta'nu ta'inu tiav'nu shichat'nu rasha'nu

מִמִּצְוֹתֶיךָ וּמִמִּשְׁפָּטֶיךָ הַטּוֹבִים וְלֹא שָׁוָה לָנוּ.

lanu shavah velo hatovim umimish'patecha mimitzvotecha

וְאַתָּה צַדִּיק עַל כָּל הַבָּא עָלֵינוּ כִּי אֱמֶת עָשִׂיתָ

asita emet ki aleinu haba kol al tzadik v'atah

וַאֲנַחְנוּ הִרְשָׁעְנוּ:

hir'sha'nu va'anachnu

ANA BEKO'ACH

אבג יתץ	אָנָּא בְּכֹחַ גְּדֻלַּת יְמִינְךָ תַּתִּיר צְרוּרָה Ana Beko'ach Gedulat Yeminecha Tatir Tzerura	חסד Sunday	1
קרע שטן	קַבֵּל רִנַּת עַמְּךָ שַׂגְּבֵנוּ טַהֲרֵנוּ נוֹרָא Kabel Rinat Amecha Sagvenu Taharenu Nora	גבורה Monday	2
נגד יכש	נָא גִבּוֹר דּוֹרְשֵׁי יִחוּדְךָ כְּבָבַת שָׁמְרֵם Na Gibor Dorshei Yichudecha Kevavat Shomrem	תפארת Tuesday	3
בטר צתג	בָּרְכֵם טַהֲרֵם רַחֲמֵי צִדְקָתְךָ תָּמִיד גָּמְלֵם Barchem Taharem Rachamei Tzidkatecha Tamid Gomlem	נצח Wednesday	4
חקב טנע	חֲסִין קָדוֹשׁ בְּרוֹב טוּבְךָ נַהֵל עֲדָתֶךָ Chasin Kadosh Berov Tuvecha Nahel Adatecha	הוד Thursday	5
יגל פזק	יָחִיד גֵּאֶה לְעַמְּךָ פְּנֵה זוֹכְרֵי קְדֻשָּׁתֶךָ Yachid Ge'eh Le'amecha Penei Zochrei Kedushatecha	יסוד Friday	6
שקו צית	שַׁוְעָתֵנוּ קַבֵּל וּשְׁמַע צַעֲקָתֵנוּ יוֹדֵעַ תַּעֲלוּמוֹת Shav'atenu Kabel Ushma Tza'akateinu Yode'a Ta'alumot	מלכות Saturday	7
	(בלחש) בָּרוּךְ שֵׁם כְּבוֹד מַלְכוּתוֹ, לְעוֹלָם וָעֶד: (silently) Baruch shem kevot malchuto le'olam va'ed		

Scanning Direction ←

First, we say the whole *Ana Beko'ach*; then we repeat the verse corresponding to the particular day, three times. According to the kabbalistic calendar, sundown is the start of the next day. Repeating this verse helps to elevate our soul.

NAFSHI YIVITICHA

Rav Isaac Luria (the Ari), explains that when a person has attained a certain level of spirituality, he or she leaves this world to reincarnate and begin work toward the next level of his or her spiritual growth. This verse helps us rise to that next level without leaving this world.

נַפְשִׁי אִוִּיתִךָ בַּלַּיְלָה מלה אַף רוּחִי בְקִרְבִּי שֹדי אֲשַׁחֲרֶךָ

ashacharecha vekir'bi ruchi af balayilah yiviticha nafshi

כִּי כַּאֲשֶׁר מִשְׁפָּטֶיךָ לָאָרֶץ צֶדֶק לָמְדוּ יֹשְׁבֵי

yoshvei lamdu tzedek la'aretz mishpatecha ka'asher ki

תֵבֵל בּ"פ רי"ו:

tevel

LAMNATZE'ACH

According to the Ari, this Psalms helps to enhance and stimulate our memory. It also helps our soul achieve its full potential by motivating us to accomplish all the spiritual work that we came to this world to do.

לַמְנַצֵּחַ מִזְמוֹר לְדָוִד: בְּבוֹא אֵלָיו נָתָן הַנָּבִיא כַּאֲשֶׁר

ka'asher hanavi natan elav bevo leDavid mizmor lamnatze'ach

בָּא אֶל בַּת שָׁבַע: חָנֵּנִי אֱלֹהִים ילה כְּחַסְדֶּךָ כְּרֹב

kerov kechasdecha Elohim chaneni shava bat el ba

רַחֲמֶיךָ מְחֵה פְשָׁעָי: הֶרֶב כַּבְּסֵנִי מֵעֲוֹנִי

me'avoni kabseni herev pesha'ai mecheh rachamecha

וּמֵחַטָּאתִי   טַהֲרֵנִי: כִּי   פְשָׁעַי   אֲנִי   אני   אֵדַע   וְחַטָּאתִי
vechatati   eda   ani   pesha'ai   ki   tahareni   umecha'tati

נֶגְדִּי   תָמִיד   נהב: לָךְ   לְבַדְּךָ   וְחַטָאתִי   וְהָרַע   בְּעֵינֶיךָ
be'einecha   vehara   chatati   levadecha   lecha   tamid   neg'di

עָשִׂיתִי   לְמַעַן   תִּצְדַּק   בְּדָבְרֶךָ   ראה   תִּזְכֶּה   בְשָׁפְטֶךָ:
veshaf'techa   tiz'keh   bedavrecha   titzedak   lema'an   asiti

הֵן   בְּעָווֹן   חוֹלָלְתִּי   וּבְחֵטְא   יֶחֱמַתְנִי   אִמִּי: הֵן   אֱמֶת
emet   hen   imi   yechemat'ni   uv'chet   cholal'ti   be'avon   hen

וְחָפַצְתָּ   בַטֻּחוֹת   וּבְסָתֻם   וְחָכְמָה   תּוֹדִיעֵנִי: תְּחַטְּאֵנִי
techateni   todi'eini   chochmah   uv'satum   batuchot   chafatzta

בְּאֵזוֹב   וְאֶטְהָר   תְּכַבְּסֵנִי   וּמִשֶּׁלֶג   אַלְבִּין: תַּשְׁמִיעֵנִי
tashmi'eni   al'bin   umisheleg   techab'seni   ve'et'har   ve'ezov

שָׂשׂוֹן   וְשִׂמְחָה   תָּגֵלְנָה   עֲצָמוֹת   דִּכִּיתָ:   הַסְתֵּר   ב"פ מצר
haster   dikita   atzamot   tagelna   vesim'chah   sasson

פָּנֶיךָ   מֵחֲטָאַי   וְכָל   עֲוֹנֹתַי   מְחֵה: לֵב   טָהוֹר   י"פ אבא
tahor   lev   mecheh   avonotai   vechol   mechata'ai   paneicha

בְּרָא   נהב   לִי   אֱלֹהִים   ילה   וְרוּחַ   נָכוֹן   חַדֵּשׁ   בְּקִרְבִּי: עדר"ג
bekirbi   chadesh   nachon   veru'ach   Elohim   li   bera

אַל   תַּשְׁלִיכֵנִי   מִלְּפָנֶיךָ   וְרוּחַ   קָדְשְׁךָ   אַל   תִּקַּח
tikach   al   kadshecha   veru'ach   mil'faneicha   tash'licheni   al

מִמֶּנִּי: הָשִׁיבָה לִּי שְׂשׂוֹן יִשְׁעֶךָ וְרוּחַ נְדִיבָה

nedivah veru'ach yish'echa sesson li hashivah mimeni

תִסְמְכֵנִי: אֲלַמְּדָה פֹשְׁעִים דְּרָכֶיךָ וְחַטָּאִים אֵלֶיךָ

eilecha vechata'im deracheicha fosh'im alamdah tismecheni

יָשׁוּבוּ: הַצִּילֵנִי מִדָּמִים אֱלֹהִים ילה אֱלֹהֵי דמב תְּשׁוּעָתִי

teshu'ati Elohei Elohim midamim hatzileni yashuvu

תָּרֶנָּן לְשׁוֹנִי צִדְקָתֶךָ: אֲדֹנָי שְׂפָתַי תִּפְתָּח וּפִי יַגִּיד יוי

yagid ufi tif'tach sefatai Adonai tzid'katecha leshoni teranen

תְהִלָּתֶךָ: כִּי לֹא תַחְפֹּץ זֶבַח וְאֶתֵּנָה נתה עוֹלָה לֹא

lo olah ve'etenah zevach tachpotz lo ki tehilatecha

תִרְצֶה: זִבְחֵי אֱלֹהִים ילה רוּחַ נִשְׁבָּרָה לֵב נִשְׁבָּר

nishbar lev nishbarah ru'ach Elohim ziv'ch tirtzeh

וְנִדְכֶּה אֱלֹהִים ילה לֹא תִבְזֶה: הֵיטִיבָה בִרְצוֹנְךָ אֶת

et vir'tzon'cha heitivah tivzeh lo Elohim venidkeh

צִיּוֹן יוֹסֵף תִּבְנֶה חוֹמוֹת נתה יְרוּשָׁלָיִם: אָז תַחְפֹּץ זִבְחֵי

zivchei tach'potz az Yerushalayim chomot tiv'neh Tzion

צֶדֶק עוֹלָה וְכָלִיל אָז יַעֲלוּ עַל מִזְבַּחֲךָ פָרִים:

parim miz'bachacha al ya'alu az vechalil olah tzedek

IM TISHKAV

These five verses act as a security deposit for our soul, guaranteeing that it will return to us in the morning.

אִם תִּשְׁכַּב לֹא תִפְחָד וְשָׁכַבְתָּ וְעָרְבָה שְׁנָתֶךְ:

shenatecha ve'arvah veshachav'ta tif'chad lo tishkav im

אַתָּה סֵתֶר בּ״פ מֵצֵר לִי מִצָּר תִּצְּרֵנִי רָנֵּי פַּלֵּט תְּסוֹבְבֵנִי

tesoveveni palet ranei titz'reni mitzar li seter atah

סֶלָה:

Selah

תּוֹדִיעֵנִי אֹרַח חַיִּים שֹׂבַע שְׂמָחוֹת אֶת פָּנֶיךָ נְעִמוֹת

ne'imot paneicha et semachot sova chayim orach todi'eni

בִּימִינְךָ נֶצַח:

netzach bi'iminecha

אַתָּה תָקוּם תְּרַחֵם אַבְרָהָם צִיּוֹן יוֹסֵף כִּי עֵת לְחֶנְנָהּ

lechen'nah et ki Tzion terachem takum ata

כִּי בָא מוֹעֵד:

mo'ed va ki

בְּיָדְךָ אַפְקִיד רוּחִי פָּדִיתָה אוֹתִי יְהוָֹהֱאדנאיהדוֹנֶהי

Adonai oti paditah ruchi afkid beyad'cha

אֵל אֱמֶת:

emet El

The *Zohar*

Specific judgments come to our world when the sun sets and night descends. At the stroke of midnight, another transformation occurs as the awesome and compassionate Light of mercy appears in the cosmos. According to the wisdom of the Kabbalah, whoever delves into the study of *Zohar* during this time of Mercy, after midnight, shall merit the protection and blessings of the Upper World.

This mystery is conveyed through a story about Rabbi Aba and Rabbi Ya'akov. The two eminent mystics are traveling through a certain village and they take up lodging at an inn. The inn-keeper has built a complex apparatus that uses water, buckets, and scales to signal the arrival of midnight. These complexities and metaphors within this seemingly simple tale indicate the extreme importance of spiritual study after the stroke of midnight.

When we study or scan this section from the *Zohar*: Lech Lecha, 34:363 – 381, after midnight, the compassionate Light of Mercy is aroused. This Light helps us access protection and blessings in our lives now, as well as receive the merit of a share in the world to come. Once again, please scan the Aramaic letters from right to left.

363. בְּפַלְגוּת לֵילְיָא, כַּד צִפֳּרִין מִתְעָרִין, סְטָרָא דְּצָפוֹן אִתְעַר בְּרוּחָא, קָם בְּקִיּוּמֵיהּ, שַׁרְבִּיטָא דִּבְסִטַר דָּרוֹם, וּבָטַע בְּהַהוּא רוּחָא, וְסָלֵיק וְאִתְבְּסַם, כְּדֵין אִתְעַר קֻדְשָׁא בְּרִיךְ הוּא בְּנִמוּסוֹי, לְאִשְׁתַּעְשְׁעָא עִם צַדִּיקַיָּא בְּגִנְּתָא דְּעֵדֶן.

363. At midnight, when the birds awaken, THAT IS, THE COCKS, a spirit (or wind) rises in the North. THIS REFERS TO THE LEFT COLUMN, WHICH IS THE SECRET OF THE ILLUMINATION OF *CHOCHMAH* WITHOUT *CHASSADIM* – THE SECRET OF THE UPPER THREE *SEFIROT* OF *RUACH*. The scepter then rises in the South, NAMELY IN THE RIGHT COLUMN, WHICH IS THE SECRET OF *CHASSADIM*, and unites with that spirit OF THE LEFT COLUMN. THUS, THEY ARE INCLUDED WITHIN EACH OTHER, AND THE JUDGMENTS OF THE LEFT COLUMN subside and are mitigated BY *CHASSADIM*. And the Holy One, blessed be He, is awakened and, as is His wont, delights Himself with the righteous in the Garden of Eden.

364. בְּהַהוּא שַׁעְתָּא, זַכָּאָה דְּקָדְשָׁא וְחוּלָקֵיהּ דְּבַר נָשׁ דְּקָאִים לְאִשְׁתַּעְשְׁעָא בְּאוֹרַיְיתָא, דְּהָא קֻדְשָׁא בְּרִיךְ הוּא, וְכָל צַדִּיקַיָּא דִּבְגִנְּתָא דְּעֵדֶן, כֻּלְּהוּ צַיְיתִין לְקָלֵיהּ. הֲדָא הוּא דִּכְתִיב הַיּוֹשֶׁבֶת בַּגַּנִּים חֲבֵרִים מַקְשִׁיבִים לְקוֹלֵךְ הַשְׁמִיעִנִי.

364. Happy is he who awakens at that time to delight in the Torah, because the Holy One, blessed be He, together with all the righteous in the Garden of Eden listen attentively to his voice. This is why it is written, "You that dwell in the gardens, the companions hearken to your voice—cause me to hear it" (*Song of Songs 8:13*).

365. וְלֹא עוֹד, אֶלָּא דְּקֻדְשָׁא בְּרִיךְ הוּא מָשֵׁיךְ עֲלֵיהּ חַד חוּטָא דְּחֶסֶד, לְמֶהֱוֵי נָטִיר בְּעָלְמָא, דְּהָא עִלָּאִין וְתַתָּאִין נָטְרִין לֵיהּ. הֲדָא הוּא דִּכְתִיב, יוֹמָם יְצַוֶּה ה' חַסְדּוֹ וּבַלַּיְלָה שִׁירֹה עִמִּי.

365. In addition, the Holy One, blessed be He, draws down upon him a thread of grace (lit. 'chesed') which earns him protection in this world from both higher and lower beings. Therefore it is written, "God will command His loving kindness (Heb. Chesed) in the daytime, and in the night His song shall be with me" (Psalms 42:9).

366. אָמַר רְבִּי חִזְקִיָּה, כָּל מַאן דְּאִשְׁתַּדַּל בְּהַאי שַׁעְתָּא בְּאוֹרַיְיתָא, וַדַּאי אִית לֵיהּ חוּלָקָא תָּדִיר בְּעָלְמָא דְאָתֵי. אָמַר ר' יוֹסֵי, מַ"טּ תָּדִיר. אָמַר לוֹ הָכֵי אוֹלִיפְנָא, דְּכָל פַּלְגוּת לֵילְיָא, כַּד קֻדְשָׁא בְּרִיךְ הוּא אִתְעַר בְּגִנְתָּא דְעֵדֶן, כָּל אִינּוּן נְטִיעָן דְּגִנְתָּא אִשְׁתַּקְיָין יַתִּיר, מֵהַהוּא נַחֲלָא, דְּאִקְרֵי נַחַל קְדוּמִים, נַחַל עֲדָנִים, דְּלָא פַּסְקוּ מֵימוֹי לְעָלְמִין, כִּבְיָכוֹל הַהוּא דְקָאִים וְאִשְׁתַּדַּל בְּאוֹרַיְיתָא, כְּאִילוּ הַהוּא נַחֲלָא אִתְרַק עַל רֵישֵׁיהּ, וְאַשְׁקֵי לֵיהּ, בְּגוֹ אִינּוּן נְטִיעָן דְּבְגִנְתָּא דְעֵדֶן.

366. Rabbi Chizkiyah said, whoever delves to the study of Torah at that hour shall definitely have an eternal share in the World to Come. Rabbi Yosi then asked, what is the meaning of 'eternal'? He answered, This is what I have learned. Every midnight, when the Holy One, blessed be He, enters the Garden of Eden, all the plants – NAMELY THE SEFIROT, of the Garden of Eden, WHICH IS THE NUKVA – are watered most generously by the stream that is called the 'ancient stream' and also the 'stream of delight,' WHICH REFERS TO THE SUPERNAL ABA AND IMA, which waters never cease to flow; BECAUSE THE MATING OF ABA AND IMA NEVER STOPS. So, if a person awakens to study Torah, it is as if that stream is poured on his head and he is watered, together with the plants of the Garden of Eden. HE RECEIVES AN ETERNAL PORTION OF THE MOCHIN OF THE WORLD TO COME AS WELL.

367. וְלָא עוֹד, אֶלָּא הוֹאִיל וְכֻלְּהוּ צַדִּיקַיָּיא, דְּבְגוֹ גִּנְתָּא דְעֵדֶן, צַיְיתִין לֵיהּ, וְחוּלָקָא שַׁוְיָין לֵיהּ, בְּהַהוּא שַׁקְיוּ דְּנַחֲלָא, אִשְׁתְּכַח דְּאִית לֵיהּ חוּלָקָא תָּדִיר, בְּעָלְמָא דְאָתֵי.

367. Furthermore, because all the righteous in the Garden of Eden listen to him, they add another portion to that flow of the stream, WHICH ARE THE MOCHIN OF SUPERNAL ABA AND IMA. Therefore he has an eternal portion in the World to Come, FOR THEY ARE INCLUDED IN THE MOCHIN OF ABA AND IMA.

368. רַבִּי אַבָּא הֲוָה אָתֵי מִטְּבֶרְיָה, לְבֵי טְרוֹנְיָא דַחֲמוֹי, וְרִ' יַעֲקֹב בְּרֵיהּ הֲוָה עִמֵּיהּ, אִעַרְעוּ בְּכְפַר טַרְשָׁא, אָמַר רִ' אַבָּא, לְמָרֵיהּ דְּבֵיתָא, אִית לוֹ מָארָא דְּבֵיתָא. אָמַר לוֹ, אֲמַאי. אָמַר לוֹ, בְּגִין דְּקָאֵימְנָא בְּפַלְגוּת לֵילְיָא מַמָּשׁ.

368. Rabbi Aba was traveling from Tiberias to Tronya, where his father-in-law lived, accompanied by his son, Rabbi Yaakov. When they decided to spend the night in the village of Tarsha, Rabbi Aba asked his landlord, "Is there a cock around here?" The landlord asked, "What do you need a cock for?" Rabbi Aba responded, "Because I awake at midnight exactly! AND I NEED A COCK TO WAKE ME UP.

369. אָמַר לוֹ, לָא אִצְטְרִיךְ, דְּהָא סִימָנָא לִי בְּבֵיתָא, דְּהַדֵּין טַקְלֵי דְּקַמֵּי עַרְסָאי, מַלְיָא לֵיהּ מַיָא, וְנָטִיף טִיף טִיף, בְּפַלְגוּת לֵילְיָא מַמָּשׁ, אִתְרְקָנוּ כֻּלְּהוֹ מַיָא, וְאִתְגַּלְגַּל הַאי קִיטְפָא, וְנָחֵים, וְאִשְׁתְּמַע קָלָא בְּכֹל בֵּיתָא, וּכְדֵין הוּא פַלְגוּת לֵילְיָא מַמָּשׁ. וְחַד סָבָא הֲוָה לִי, דַּהֲוָה קָם בְּכֹל פַלְגוּת לֵילְיָא, וְאִשְׁתַּדַּל בְּאוֹרַיְיתָא, וּבְגִינֵי כָךְ, עָבַד הַאי.

369. THE LANDLORD then said, You do not need THE COCK. I have prepared a signal in the house that indicates midnight, the scales that are before my bed. For this purpose, I fill a vessel with water. The water drips out THROUGH A HOLE IN THE VESSEL so that it empties exactly at midnight. AT THAT MOMENT, ONE SCALE GOES UP WHILE THE OTHER swings downward and roars. IT MAKES NOISE AS IT FALLS. And the sound is heard throughout the house. The signal was created by an old man who once stayed with me and arose at exactly midnight to study Torah.

370. אָמַר רִ' אַבָּא, בְּרִיךְ רַחֲמָנָא דְּשַׁדְּרַנִי דְּשַׁדְּרַנִי הָכָא. בְּפַלְגוּת לֵילְיָא נָהֵם, הַהוּא גַּלְגּוּלָא דְּקִיטְפָא, קָמוּ רַבִּי אַבָּא וְרַבִּי יַעֲקֹב. שָׁמְעוּ לְהַהוּא גַּבְרָא, דַּהֲוָה יָתִיב בְּשִׁיפּוּלֵי בֵּיתָא, וּתְרֵין בְּנוֹי עִמֵּיהּ, וַהֲוָה אָמַר, כְּתִיב וְחֲצוֹת לַיְלָה אָקוּם לְהוֹדוֹת לָךְ עַל מִשְׁפְּטֵי צִדְקֶךָ, מַאי קָא וְזִמְנָא דְּוִד, דְּאִיהוּ אָמַר וְחֲצוֹת לַיְלָה, וְלָא בַּחֲצוֹת לַיְלָה. אֶלָּא, וַדַּאי לְקוּדְשָׁא בְּרִיךְ הוּא אָמַר הָכִי.

370. Rabbi Aba said, Blessed be God, the Merciful, who has sent me over here. At midnight, the scale made a noise as it swung down, waking Rabbi Aba and Rabbi Ya'akov. They heard their landlord, who was sitting in a corner of the house with his two sons, say, "It is written, 'Midnight I will rise to give thanks to You because of Your righteous judgments'" (*Psalms 119:62*). AND HE ASKED, "What did David see that caused him to say 'Midnight...'" instead of "at midnight...?" AND HE REPLIES, Most certainly he was referring to the Holy One, blessed be He, CALLING Him 'MIDNIGHT.'

371. וְכִי קֻדְשָׁא בְּרִיךְ הוּא הָכֵי אִקְרֵי. אֵין, דְּהָא וְצוֹת לַיְלָה מַמָּשׁ, קֻדְשָׁא בְּרִיךְ הוּא אִשְׁתְּכַח, וְסִיעָתָא דִּילֵיהּ, וּכְדֵין אִיהוּ שַׁעֲתָא דְּעָיֵיל בְּגִנְתָא דְּעֵדֶן, לְאִשְׁתַּעְשְׁעָא עִם צַדִּיקַיָּא.

371. AND HE ASKS, Is the Holy One, blessed be He, called so? HE ANSWERED, Yes! Because at midnight exactly, the Holy One, blessed be He, appears with His retinue, and enters the Garden of Eden to delight with the righteous.

372. אָמַר רִבִּי אַבָּא, לְרִבִּי יַעֲקֹב, וַדַּאי נִשְׁתַּתַּף בִּשְׁכִינְתָּא, וְנִתְחַבַּר כַּחֲדָא, קָרִיבוּ וְיָתִיבוּ עִמֵּיהּ, אָמְרוּ לֵיהּ, אֵימָא מִלָּה דִּפוּמָךְ, דְּשַׁפִּיר קָאָמְרַתְּ. מְנָא לָךְ הַאי. אָמַר לוֹן, מִלָּה דָּא, אוֹלִיפְנָא מִסָּבָאי.

372. Rabbi Aba said to Rabbi Yaakov, "We shall surely join the *Shechinah*, so let us join THAT MAN AND HIS SONS." They came closer, sat with him, and said, Say whatever you have to say, for you have spoken well! THEY ASKED HIM, From where do you know all this? He responded, I have learned this from my grandfather.

373. וְתוּ הֲוָה אָמַר, דְּתְחוֹלַת שַׁעֲתֵי קַדְמָאֵיתָא דְּלֵילְיָא, כָּל דִּינִין דִּלְתַתָּא מִתְעָרִין, וְאַזְלִין וְשָׁאטִין בְּעָלְמָא. בְּפַלְגוּת לֵילְיָא מַמָּשׁ, קֻדְשָׁא בְּרִיךְ הוּא אִתְּעַר בְּגִנְתָא דְּעֵדֶן, וְדִינִין דִּלְתַתָּא לָא מִשְׁתַּכְּחִין.

373. And he continued, At the first hour of the night all the judgments down below are aroused, THE JUDGMENTS OF *MALCHUT* WHICH ARE NOT SWEETENED BY *BINAH*, and fly around the world. Exactly at midnight, however, when the Holy One,

blessed be He, enters the Garden of Eden, WHICH IS THE *NUKVA*, these Judgments disappear and cease to exist.

374. וְכָל נִימוּסִין דִּלְעֵילָּא, בְּלֵילְיָא לָא אִשְׁתַּכְחוּ, אֶלָּא בְּפַלְגּוּת לֵילְיָא מַמָּשׁ. מְנָלָן, מֵאַבְרָהָם, דִּכְתִיב וַיֵּחָלֵק עֲלֵיהֶם לַיְלָה. בְּמִצְרַיִם, וַיְהִי בַּחֲצִי הַלַּיְלָה. וּבְאַתְרִין סַגִּיאִין בְּאוֹרַיְיתָא הָכִי אִשְׁתַּכְחוּ. וְדָוִד הֲוָה יָדַע.

374. And all the pathways of above – NAMELY THE WAYS BY WHICH *BINAH* SWEETENS THE *NUKVA* – only occur exactly at midnight. How do we know this? We know this from the verse about Abraham, "And he divided himself against them... (by) night" (*Genesis 14:15*). But in Egypt, IT IS WRITTEN, "And it came to pass at midnight" (*Exodus 12:29*) BECAUSE THE *NUKVA* WAS THEN SWEETENED BY *BINAH* AND HER LIGHT WAS REVEALED. And David knew of this, WHICH IS WHY HE SAID, "MIDNIGHT."

375. וּמְנָא הֲוָה יָדַע. אֶלָּא, הָכִי אֲמַר סָבָא, דְּמַלְכוּתָא דִּילֵיהּ בְּהַאי תַּלְיָא. וְעַל דָּא קָאִים בְּהַהִיא שַׁעֲתָא, וַאֲמַר שִׁירָתָא, וּלְהָכִי קָרֵיהּ לְקֻדְשָׁא בְּרִיךְ הוּא וַחֲצוֹת לַיְלָה מַמָּשׁ אָקוּם לְהוֹדוֹת לָךְ וְגוֹ'. דְּהָא כָּל דִּינִין תַּלְיָין מֵהָכָא, וְדִינִין דְּמַלְכוּתָא מֵהָכָא מִשְׁתַּכְּחִין וַהֲהִיא שַׁעֲתָא, אִתְקַטַּר בָּהּ דָּוִד, וְקָם. וַאֲמַר שִׁירָתָא. אָתָא רַבִּי אַבָּא וּנְשָׁקֵיהּ, אָמַר לוֹ וַדַּאי הָכִי הוּא, בְּרִיךְ רַחֲמָנָא, דְּשַׁדְּרַנִי הָכָא.

375. AND HE ASKED, "How did DAVID know this?" AND HE ANSWERED, so said my grandfather. Because his Kingdom OF DAVID depended on this, ON THE ILLUMINATION OF THE *MOCHIN* OF MIDNIGHT, David therefore rose at midnight and chanted songs. And so he actually called the Holy One, blessed be He, "Midnight." He also said, "I will rise to give thanks to You..." Then, at that hour, all Judgments stem from here, MEANING ONLY FROM THE *NUKVA* WHICH IS SWEETENED AT MIDNIGHT, AS THE JUDGMENTS OF THE WORLD BELOW HAVE ALREADY DISAPPEARED. So the Judgments of *Malchut* are derived only from here, AND NOT FROM ITS UNSWEETENED ASPECT. Therefore, at that hour, David attached himself to it and rose up to chant songs. Rabbi Aba went forward and kissed him. He said, "It is assuredly so! Blessed be the Merciful One, who has brought me here."

376 . תָּא חֲזֵי, לֵילְיָא דִּינָא בְּכָל אֲתַר, וְהָא אוּקִימְנָא מִלָּה, וְהָכֵי הוּא וַדַּאי, וְהָא אִתְּעַר קַמֵּי דְּרַבִּי שִׁמְעוֹן. אָמַר הַהוּא יְנוּקָא, בְּרֵיהּ דְּהַהוּא גַּבְרָא, אִי הָכֵי, אֲמַאי כְּתִיב וַחֲצוֹת לַיְלָה. אָמַר לוֹ, הָא אִתְּמַר, בְּפַלְגוּת לֵילְיָא, מַלְכוּתָא דִּשְׁמַיָּא אִתְּעָרַת. אָמַר אֲנָא שְׁמַעְנָא מִלָּה. אָמַר לוֹ, ר' אַבָּא, אֵימָא בְּרִי טַב דְּהָא מִלָּה דְּפוּמָךְ, קָלָא דְּבוֹצִינָא לֶהֱוֵי.

376. Come and behold, As we have already explained, "night" has always been the time of Judgment; it was discussed in the presence of Rabbi Shimon and is certainly so! The young son of the landlord then asked, "If so, then why is it written, 'Midnight'?" They explained to him, "It is as we have already stated, because the Kingdom of Heaven is awakened at midnight." The son said, I have heard that, but have another explanation! Rabbi Aba then said, Well then, speak up, my son! For your words shall be the voice of the candle, REFERRING TO THE VOICE OF RABBI SHIMON, WHO IS CALLED THE 'LUMINOUS LIGHT.'

377 . אָמַר, אֲנָא שְׁמַעְנָא, דְּהָא לֵילְיָא דִּינָא דְּמַלְכוּתָא אִיהוּ, וּבְכָל אֲתַר דִּינָא הוּא, וְהַאי דְּקָאָמַר וַחֲצוֹת, בְּגִין דְּיָנְקָא בִּתְרֵי גַוְונֵי, בְּדִינָא וּבְחֶסֶד, וַדַּאי פַּלְגוּתָא קַדְמָאֵיתָא, דִּינָא הוּא, דְּהָא פַּלְגוּתָא אָחֳרָא, נְהִירוּ אַנְפָּהָא בְּסִטְרָא דְּחֶסֶד. וְעַל דָּא וַחֲצוֹת לַיְלָה כְּתִיב וַדַּאי.

377. THE YOUNG SON said, I heard that the night is the time when the Judgment of Malchut is in power. As a result, everywhere THE TERM 'NIGHT' APPEARS, it refers to Judgment. But when the term midnight appears, it is because Malchut is nourished from the two aspects – Judgment and Chesed. So, the first half of the night is the time of Judgment. During the second half, however, the face shines from the aspect of Chesed. This is why it is written, 'Midnight' – THE HALF OF CHESED.

378 . קָם רַבִּי אַבָּא, וְשַׁוֵּי יְדוֹי בְּרֵישֵׁיהּ, וּבָרְכֵיהּ, אָמַר וַדַּאי, וְשֵׁיזָבְנָא דְּחָכְמְתָא לָא אִשְׁתְּכַח בַּר בְּאִינוּן זַכָּאֵי דְּזָכוֹ בָּהּ. הַשְׁתָּא וַזְמַנָא, דְּאֲפִילוּ יְנוּקֵי בְּדָרָא דְּרַבִּי שִׁמְעוֹן, זָכוֹ לְחָכְמְתָא עִלָּאָה. זַכָּאָה אַנְתְּ רַבִּי שִׁמְעוֹן. וַוי לְדָרָא דְּאַנְתְּ תִּסְתַּלַּק מִנֵּיהּ. יָתְבוּ עַד צַפְרָא. וְאִשְׁתַּדְּלוּ בְּאוֹרַיְתָא.

378. Rabbi Aba stood up, placed his hands over his head, and blessed him. He said, I thought that Wisdom was found only among the righteous, who earned it THROUGH PIOUS DEEDS. But now I see that in the generation of Rabbi Shimon, even the young have merited the Supernal Wisdom because of him. Happy are you, Rabbi Shimon. Woe to the generation from which you shall depart. They sat until the morning studying Torah.

379. פָּתַח ר' אַבָּא וְאָמַר, וְעַמֵּךְ כֻּלָּם צַדִּיקִים וְגו'. מִלָּה דָּא הָא אוֹקְמוּהָ חַבְרַיָּיא, מ"ט, כְּתִיב, וְעַמֵּךְ כֻּלָּם צַדִּיקִים, וְכִי כֻּלְּהוּ יִשְׂרָאֵל צַדִּיקֵי נִינְהוּ. וְהָא כַּמָּה וַיָּיבִין אִית בְּהוּ בְּיִשְׂרָאֵל, כַּמָּה חַטָּאִין, וְכַמָּה רְשִׁיעִין, דְּעַבְרִין עַל פִּקּוּדֵי אוֹרַיְיתָא.

379. Rabbi Aba began the discussion with the verse, "Your people also shall be all righteous..." (*Isaiah 60:21*). Our friends have already explained this passage. Why is it written, "Your people also shall be all righteous?" How can it be that all the nation of Israel is righteous, when there are many wicked people in Israel? Many are sinners and transgressors, who disobey the precepts of Torah!

380. אֶלָּא, הָכִי תָּנָא בְּרָזָא דְּמַתְנִיתִין, זַכָּאִין אִינּוּן יִשְׂרָאֵל, דְּעַבְדִין קָרְבְּנָא דִּרְעוּתָא לְקֻדְשָׁא בְּרִיךְ הוּא, דִּמְקָרְבִין בְּנַיְיהוּ יוֹמִין לִתְמַנְיָא לְקָרְבְּנָא, וְכַד אִתְגְּזָרוּ, עָאלוּ בְּהַאי חוּלָקָא טָבָא דְּקֻדְשָׁא בְּרִיךְ הוּא, דִּכְתִיב וְצַדִּיק יְסוֹד עוֹלָם. כֵּיוָן דְּעָאלוּ בְּהַאי חוּלָקָא דְּצַדִּיק, אִקְרוּן צַדִּיקִים, וַדַּאי כֻּלָּם צַדִּיקִים.

380. But the meaning is found in the secret of the Mishnah. Happy are the people of Israel, who voluntarily offer a sacrifice to the Holy One, blessed be He. The sacrifice is the circumcision of their sons eight days after birth. When they are circumcised, they take part in the good portion of the Holy One, blessed be He, as it is written, "The righteous are the foundation (Heb. *yesod*) of the world" (*Proverbs 10:25*). As they enter to this portion of the righteous, AS A RESULT OF THEIR CIRCUMCISION, they are the called "righteous." Therefore they are certainly all righteous, BECAUSE NOW THEY ARE ALL CIRCUMCISED, EVEN THE WICKED AMONG THEM. THEREFORE, IT IS WRITTEN, "YOUR PEOPLE ALSO SHALL BE ALL RIGHTEOUS..."

381. וְעַל כֵּן לְעוֹלָם יִירְשׁוּ אָרֶץ. כְּדִכְתִיב פִּתְחוּ לִי שַׁעֲרֵי צֶדֶק אָבֹא בָם. וּכְתִיב זֶה הַשַּׁעַר לַהֹ צַדִּיקִים יָבֹאוּ בוֹ. אִינוּן דְּאִתְגְּזָרוּ, וְאִקְרוּן צַדִּיקִים. נֵצֶר מַטָּעַי. נֵצֶר מֵאִינוּן נְטִיעִין דְּנָטַע קוּדְשָׁא בְּרִיךְ הוּא בְּגִנְתָּא דְּעֵדֶן, הַאי אֶרֶץ חַד מִנַּיְיהוּ, וְעַל כֵּן אִית לְהוֹ לְיִשְׂרָאֵל חוּלָקָא טָבָא, בְּעָלְמָא דְּאָתֵי. וּכְתִיב צַדִּיקִים יִירְשׁוּ אָרֶץ. לְעוֹלָם יִירְשׁוּ אָרֶץ. מַהוּ לְעוֹלָם. כְּמָה דְּאוּקִימְנָא בְּמַתְנִיתָא דִּילָן, וְהָא אִתְּמָר הַאי מִלָּה בֵּין חַבְרַיָּיא.

381. Therefore, "they shall inherit the land for ever" (*Isaiah 60:21*). THIS ALLUDES TO THE *SHECHINAH* THAT IS CALLED "THE LAND." As it is written, "Open to me the gates of righteousness, I will go through them" (*Psalms 118:19*) and "This is the gate of Hashem, through which the righteous shall enter" (*Ibid. 20*). These are those who are circumcised and are called "righteous." "The branch of my plantings" is a branch of the plantings that the Holy One, blessed be He, planted in the Garden of Eden. And this "land" is one of those plantings. THE "PLANTINGS" ARE THE *TEN SEFIROT* OF THE GARDEN OF EDEN, AND *MALCHUT* OF THEM IS CALLED "THE LAND." Therefore, the children of Israel have a goodly portion in the World to Come. As it is written, "The righteous shall inherit the land" (*Psalms 37:29*) – "they shall inherit the land forever." AND HE ASKED, "What is "forever"? AND HE SAID, Just as it is explained in our *Mishnah* and has been settled among the friends.

MORE BOOKS THAT CAN HELP YOU BRING THE WISDOM OF KABBALAH INTO YOUR LIFE

Nano: Technology of Mind over Matter
By Rav Berg

Kabbalah is all about attaining control over the physical world, including our personal lives, at the most fundamental level of reality. It's about achieving and extending mind over matter and developing the ability to create fulfillment, joy, and happiness by controlling everything at the most basic level of existence. In this way, Kabbalah predates and presages the most exciting trend in recent scientific and technological development, the application of nanotechnology to all areas of life in order to create better, stronger, and more efficient results.

Immortality: The Inevitability of Eternal Life
By Rav Berg

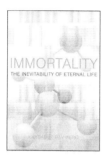

This book will totally change the way in which you perceive the world, if you simply approach its contents with an open mind and an open heart.

Most people have it backwards, dreading and battling what they see as the inevitability of aging and death. But, according to the great Kabbalist Rav Berg and the ancient wisdom of Kabbalah, it is eternal life that is inevitable.

With a radical shift in our cosmic awareness and the transformation of the collective consciousness that will follow, we can bring about the demise of the death force once and for all—in this "lifetime."

www.kabbalah.com

Days of Connection: A Guide to Kabbalah's Holidays and New Moons
By Michael Berg

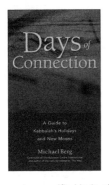

The ancient wisdom of Kabbalah teaches that each month of the lunar year holds different opportunities for us to grow and change and, conversely, holds unique pitfalls for getting stalled on our journey toward spiritual transformation. The special power of each month is strongest at its beginning, the time of the new moon, known as Rosh Chodesh. And holidays are unmatched as windows in time that make specific kinds of spiritual energy available to us. In *Days of Connection*, Michael Berg guides us through the kabbalistic calendar and explains the meaning and power behind all of these special days.

Angel Intelligence
By Yehuda Berg

Discover how billions of angels exist and shape the world, and how, through your thoughts and deeds, you have the power to create them, whether positive or negative. You'll learn their individual names and characteristics and their unique roles, as well as how to call on them for different purposes and use them as powerful spiritual tools for transformation. By becoming aware of the angel dynamics at work in the universe and by learning how to connect with these unseen energy forces, you will gain amazing insight and the ability to meet life's greatest challenges.

The Power of Kabbalah
By Yehuda Berg

Imagine your life filled with unending joy, purpose, and contentment. Imagine your days infused with pure insight and energy. This is *The Power of Kabbalah*. It is the path from the momentary pleasure that most of us settle for, to the lasting fulfillment that is yours to claim. Your deepest desires are waiting to be realized. Find out how, in this basic introduction to the ancient wisdom of Kabbalah.

www.kabbalah.com

The Dreams Book: Finding Your Way in the Dark
By Yehuda Berg

Lift the curtain of reality and discover the secrets of dream interpretation that have remained hidden for centuries. Learn powerful techniques to attract soul mates, improve relationships, recognize career opportunities, and much more. This book holds the key to navigating the dreamscape, where the answers to life's questions are revealed.

Kabbalah on Pain: How to Use It to Lose It
By Yehuda Berg

Learn how to use your emotional pain to your advantage and how to release its grip on you forever. When you avoid, ignore, or bury your pain, you only prolong psychic agony. But Kabbalah teaches a method for detaching from the source of this pain—human ego—and thereby forcing ego to take on and deal with your pain. When you choose the path of the soul where only ego suffers, you will begin to move toward the state of pure joy that is your destiny.

God Does Not Create Miracles, You Do!
By Yehuda Berg

Stop waiting for a miracle and start making miracles happen! Discover powerful tools to help you break free of whatever is standing between you and the complete happiness you deserve. This book gives you the formula for creating the connection with the true source of miracles that lies only within yourself.

Kabbalah on the Sabbath
By Yehuda Berg

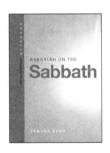

According to Kabbalah, the period between Friday sunset and Saturday sunset is very different from, and more important than, any of the other days of the week. Kabbalists believe that the Sabbath is the only day when the spiritual and physical worlds are united, making it the most powerful day. The Light force flows continually, giving the opportunity to refuel energy and rejuvenate the soul for the coming week. But, the day is not one of rest, nor is it about worship; it's about making a connection, which takes spiritual work. This book clearly explains how to make that connection.

THE ZOHAR

Composed more than 2,000 years ago, the *Zohar* is a set of 23 books, a commentary on biblical and spiritual matters in the form of conversations among spiritual masters. But to describe the *Zohar* only in physical terms is greatly misleading. In truth, the *Zohar* is nothing less than a powerful tool for achieving the most important purposes of our lives. It was given to all humankind by the Creator to bring us protection, to connect us with the Creator's Light, and ultimately to fulfill our birthright of true spiritual transformation.

More than eighty years ago, when The Kabbalah Centre was founded, the *Zohar* had virtually disappeared from the world. Few people in the general population had ever heard of it. Whoever sought to read it—in any country, in any language, at any price— faced a long and futile search.

Today all this has changed. Through the work of The Kabbalah Centre and the editorial efforts of Michael Berg, the *Zohar* is now being brought to the world, not only in the original Aramaic language but also in English. The new English *Zohar* provides everything for connecting to this sacred text on all levels: the original Aramaic text for scanning; an English translation; and clear, concise commentary for study and learning.

THE KABBALAH CENTRE®

The Kabbalah Centre® is a spiritual organization dedicated to bringing the wisdom of Kabbalah to the world. The Kabbalah Centre® itself has existed for more than 80 years, but its spiritual lineage extends back to Rav Isaac Luria in the 16th century and even further back to Rav Shimon bar Yochai, who revealed the principal text of Kabbalah, the Zohar, more than 2,000 years ago.

The Kabbalah Centre® was founded in 1922 by Rav Yehuda Ashlag, one of the greatest kabbalists of the 20th Century. When Rav Ashlag left this world, leadership of The Kabbalah Centre® was taken on by Rav Yehuda Brandwein. Before his passing, Rav Brandwein designated Rav Berg as director of The Kabbalah Centre®. Now, for more than 30 years, The Kabbalah Centre® has been under the direction of Rav Berg, his wife Karen Berg, and their sons, Yehuda Berg and Michael Berg.

Although there are many scholarly studies of Kabbalah, The Kabbalah Centre® does not teach Kabbalah as an academic discipline but as a way of creating a better life. The mission of The Kabbalah Centre® is to make the practical tools and spiritual teachings of Kabbalah available and accessible to everyone regardless of religion, ethnicity, gender or age.

The Kabbalah Centre® makes no promises. But if people are willing to work hard to grow and become actively sharing, caring and tolerant human beings, Kabbalah teaches that they will then experience fulfillment and joy in a way previously unknown to them. This sense of fulfillment, however, comes gradually and is always the result of the student's spiritual work.

Our ultimate goal is for all humanity to gain the happiness and fulfillment that is our true destiny.

Kabbalah teaches its students to question and test everything they learn. One of the most important teachings of Kabbalah is that there is no coercion in spirituality.

What Does The Kabbalah Centre® Offer?

Local Kabbalah Centres around the world offer onsite lectures, classes, study groups, holiday celebrations and services, and a community of teachers and fellow students. To find a Centre near you, go to www.kabbalah.com.

For those of you unable to access a physical Kabbalah Centre due to the constraints of location or time, we have other ways to participate in The Kabbalah Centre® community.

At www.kabbalah.com, we feature online blogs, newsletters, weekly wisdom, a store, and much more.

It's a wonderful way to stay tuned in and in touch, and it gives you access to programs that will expand your mind and challenge you to continue your spiritual work.

Student Support

The Kabbalah Centre® empowers people to take responsibility for their own lives. It's about the teachings, not the teachers. But on your journey to personal growth, things can be unclear and sometimes rocky, so it is helpful to have a coach or teacher. Simply call 1 800 KABBALAH toll free.

All Student Support instructors have studied Kabbalah under the direct supervision of Kabbalist Rav Berg, widely recognized as the preeminent kabbalist of our time.

We have also created opportunities for you to interact with other Student Support students through study groups, monthly connections, holiday retreats, and other events held around the country.

To everyone, everywhere,

May the wisdom of Kabbalah hold you tight,
as you hold on with all your heart, mind,
body and soul.

Rachel Salazar